THE COMPLETE GUIDE TO ADOPTING A CAT

Laura Cassiday

www.lpmedia.org

Publication Data

Laura Cassiday

The Complete Guide to Adopting a Cat – First edition.

Summary: "Preparing for, Selecting, Raising, Training, and Loving Your New Adopted Cat or Kitten"

– Provided by publisher.

ISBN: 978-1-954288-34-8

[1. Cat Care – Non-Fiction] I. Title.

This book has been written with the published intent to provide accurate and author-itative information in regard to the subject matter included. While every reasonable precaution has been taken in preparation of this book the author and publisher expressly disclaim responsibility for any errors, omissions, or adverse effects arising from the use or application of the information contained inside. The techniques and suggestions are to be used at the reader's discretion and are not to be considered a substitute for professional veterinary care. If you suspect a medical problem with your cat, consult your veterinarian.

Design by Sorin Rădulescu

First paperback edition, 2021

TABLE OF CONTENTS

PREFACE 1

CHAPTER 1
Choosing a Cat 3
What Type of Cat Fits Your Lifestyle? 3
    Age – Kitten, Adult, Senior? 4
    Breed 5
    Gender 6
    How Many? 6
Indoor, Outdoor, or Indoor/Outdoor? 7
Considering "Different" or "Special Needs" Cats 11
The Facts about Declawing 12
The Benefits of Spay/Neuter 13

CHAPTER 2
Rescue vs. Shelter vs. Private Owner: How Do I Choose? . . . 19
Shelters 20
Rescues 22
Why Do I Need to Pay an Adoption Fee? AKA the Myth of the "Free Kitten" 25
Why Do I Need to Complete an Application? 27

CHAPTER 3
The Two Sides of Rehoming 33
What to Do if You've Found a Stray Cat or Kittens 33
Obtaining a Cat from a Private Owner 39
How to Identify a Scam/Red Flags 42
The Problem with Pet Shops 42
Responsible Rehoming: When It Just Doesn't Work Out 43

CHAPTER 4

Becoming a Cat Foster Parent 49

Why Are Foster Parents Needed? 50

How Do I Become a Foster Parent? 50

Questions to Ask the Rescue or Shelter 52

Isn't It Difficult to Give Them Up? 56

CHAPTER 5

Bringing Kitty Home 61

What Supplies Do I Need? 61

Setting Up a Safe Space 67

The Two-Week Shutdown 68

Understanding Cat Body Language 73

Introductions to Kids, Dogs, Other Cats, and Other Pets   75

CHAPTER 6

Nutrition and Health Care 85

Feeding Your Cat 86

First Vet Visit and How to Find a Vet 92

Preventative Health Care 94

How Do You Know When It's Time for the Vet? 97

Grooming and Shedding 99

CHAPTER 7

Troubleshooting Problems 103

Positive Reinforcement Works 103

Litter Box Issues 106

Destructive Scratching 114

Biting and Aggression 117

Fear and Anxiety 124

Nuisance Behaviors (Counter Surfing, Excessive Meowing,
and More) 127

Carrier Training 130

Giving Medication 133

CHAPTER 8

Playtime and Enrichment 135

Play Therapy 135
Food Puzzles 138
Outdoor Enrichment 141
Vertical Space 144

CHAPTER 9

Saying Goodbye: A Lifetime Commitment 149

Senior Cat Care 152
   Common Senior Cat Health Problems: 153
   Accommodating Your Senior Cat 157
End of Life and Hospice Care: How Do You Know When It's Time? . . 158
Dealing with Loss 162
Epilogue 166

PREFACE

So, you've decided to adopt a cat. Easy, right? You just go to the closest shelter, pick out the cute, fluffy, orange one, and live happily ever after.

Although this is exactly what goes through the minds of many would-be cat adopters, picking out your new best friend can be a little more complicated. I mean, if you get a kitten, you're looking at a 15-20 year commitment. I once had one of my cats live to be 27! And what happens if the cat doesn't like your other pets? Or your kids? What if it stops using its litter box? And how often do cats even need to go to the vet, anyway? Cat adoption comes with a lot of considerations that people overlook.

That's where this book comes in. It's a comprehensive guide to all things cat adoption. If you don't know where to start, this is a good place. If you've just brought your new kitty home and have questions, we'll cover that too. Even if you've already had a cat for a while, you're guaranteed to learn something new. So, grab your catnip and feather wand, and let's get started!

Common Misconceptions about Cats

Let's take a look first at some common misconceptions about cats. Why would you want one anyway? Dogs are friendlier, more loyal, and super loving, right? Cats are independent and cold. They keep to themselves. Right?

Not exactly. Cats are not dogs. This is very true. While humans domesticated dogs, cats actually domesticated themselves. About 8,000 years ago, when humans were transitioning from traveling hunter-gatherers into sedentary farmers, rodents in the area rejoiced as they now had villages full of people who grew crops and kept grain stores. Following the rodents came, of course, cats. Although the villagers weren't really interested in keeping cats as pets, they didn't mind them hanging around and preying on the rodents that destroyed their harvest. Over time, cats were essentially "tolerated" into tameness by humans and became the domestic shorthair cats you see in modern times.

This is the root cause of why cats get a bad rap over dogs. Their relationship with us as humans was entirely created by them, not us. We're just along for the ride. It's our job now to understand how they communicate with us, not the other way around.

Here are a few things people commonly believe about cats that need some clarification:

 **Cats are low maintenance.**

Wrong! Cats often fool us into thinking this due to their somewhat aloof nature. However, they have many needs, from physical and mental enrichment, to annual vet care, to companionship with people and other pets.

 **Cats are mean.**

I would argue that cats are misunderstood. A mean cat is just an unhappy or stressed cat. We'll cover more about how to recognize signs of anxiety and stress later on.

 **Cats are independent.**

In the wild, cats live in colonies, rarely on their own. Most cats don't enjoy being alone all the time and appreciate human and feline (and sometimes canine) companionship. Cats show their affection in more subtle ways than dogs do – with a slow blink or just by sitting in the same room with you, for example.

 **I just don't understand cats.**

Cats communicate to us all the time; we just don't know how to listen. Humans are quick to put labels on cats. "That cat is aggressive" or "that cat just hates me." We should be looking at the why instead. What is that cat trying to tell us by that behavior? I'll teach you how to read cat body language in this book.

CHAPTER 1

Choosing a Cat

What Type of Cat Fits Your Lifestyle?

Now that we've discredited any reasons why you wouldn't want a cat, let's talk about things to consider before you make the big leap into adoption. In order to set yourself (and the cat) up for success, you need to decide what type of cat would be a good fit. The good news is that if you're prepared and know what to look for, there's a cat out there that will fit just about any type of lifestyle! Most people walk into the shelter building or pull up Petfinder.com and ooh and ahh over the cute cats who are reaching through the bars of the cage at you or playing with string in their photo. Or they go in absolutely dead set on a black male kitten and are unwilling to compromise

Photo Courtesy
of Lisa Flanery

3

– even though they can't quite say why they want that kitten exactly. They just want a black one, and that's that. I'm asking you to make a more educated decision than that.

Age – Kitten, Adult, Senior?

Everyone wants a kitten. The reason is obvious. They're adorable. They have teeny tiny little paws and whiskers, and they make those sweatshirts with the kangaroo pouches in them, and you can carry

FUN FACT
Gender Colors

Did you know that almost all calico cats are females? In order to have the distinctive tri-color calico pattern, a cat needs to have two X chromosomes, which also dictates the gender of the cat as a female. A male cat can be born calico, but it is extremely rare. On the other hand, four out of every five orange tabby cats you see are male. This is due to only needing the "orange gene" on one chromosome, whereas females need it on both in order to have this distinctive coloring.

them around. According to an analysis of Petfinder.com adoptions by Priceonomics, 82 percent of kittens entering shelters in the United States get adopted. After 18 months of age, the percentage of cats making it out drastically drops to just 60 percent. If saving a life is important to you when it comes to adoption, you'll make more of an impact with an adult cat.

Kittens can also be little terrors. Trust me; I've had about 100 foster kittens over the last couple of years. Not everyone needs a kitten. Most of the time, when I hand off kittens to their new families, I am hiding my evil laugh behind my hands. They never have any idea what they're getting themselves into. But if you are set on adopting a kitten, you'll want to get two, and I won't budge on that. More on that later.

Think about your lifestyle before deciding on an age. Do you work a lot? Are you always home or never home? Do you have the energy to keep up with a young cat, or are you looking for a buddy to snuggle on the couch? Do you already have pets at home? If you're home a decent amount and are interested in a pet that takes a little more work, sure, get some kittens. However, if you already have an adult or senior cat, are you sure that cat also wants a kitten? Usually, cats get along best if they're similar in age. A kitten may terrorize your 13-year-old that just wants to snooze in the sunshine. If you're gone for 12 hours a day, you may want an older cat that can take care of itself. Cats can live between 15 and 20 years, so take a chance on that 10 or 12-year-old if you need a snuggle buddy who will sit in your lap all afternoon.

The obvious perk to adopting an adult or senior cat instead of a kitten is personality. All kittens are the same – cute and playful. You don't know if that kitten will grow up to be independent or attached to you at the hip. Will he be a lap cat, or will you be lucky if he allows you to pet him at all? Yes, how cats are raised plays into these traits, but much of their personality is genetic and develops over time. When you adopt an adult cat, you know what you're getting, plain and simple.

Breed

Generally, if you're thinking adoption, there's pretty much just one breed to choose from: the domestic shorthair. This is your average, run-of-the-mill kind of cat. They come in all colors, shapes, and sizes and are the "mutts" of the cat world. If you're lucky, you may find a domestic longhair or medium hair, which just means they have a longer coat than their shorthair cousins. Domestic cats all have unique personalities and characteristics, and you're sure to find whatever you're looking for in the breed.

If you're set on a purebred cat but prefer to adopt, it's definitely possible but more difficult. Breed-specific and purebred-only rescue groups exist and are prevalent no matter where you live. In my time working at shelters

Photo Courtesy of Fagan Yusifli

and with rescues, I have seen quite a few Bengals, Persians, Maine Coons, and even a Devon Rex and a Sphynx come through. With any special breed, be sure to do your research in advance and never adopt based on cuteness alone. Yes, Persians have beautiful, gorgeous smooshy faces, but did you know they commonly have issues breathing and eating? Bengals need extra enrichment and exercise beyond what many cat owners are prepared for and are prone to litter box issues or aggression if their needs are not being met. Preparation and research are key before deciding if a certain breed is a must-have for you.

Gender

Ahh, the old boys versus girls debate. I've heard arguments for and against both. The truth is it really doesn't matter. Some will say males are more aggressive, or they are more likely to spray. I've heard both that female cats are more loving and that they're more feisty. These are all inaccurate stereotypes. I do find that male/female or male/male pairs are better match-ups than female/female if you have multiple cats. Cats generally form a matriarchal community where the most dominant female is in charge, so you're better off with just one girl to minimize any arguments.

How Many?

Single kitten syndrome is what happens when you only have one kitten in your house and no other cats. It's a cute name that summarizes a big problem. To make a long story short, kittens need other kittens for healthy development. If a kitten grows up alone, it can cause behavior issues such as destruction, aggression, neediness, and more. Kittens that grow up along-side a littermate tend to be healthier, happier, and better socialized.

REASONS TO ADOPT TWO KITTENS:

- Heard anyone say that cats are solitary and independent? They were wrong! Cats naturally live in colonies, and the majority of them are happier having another kitty companion. Kittens NEED other kittens for healthy social development. Even loving, caring humans are not adequate substitutes for kitten companionship.

- Kittens are like having babies! They require constant attention and supervision. They get into things they're not supposed to without proper enrichment and stimulation. Want your kitten to stop chewing plants, climbing your curtains, using the furniture as a jungle gym, unrolling your toilet paper, and eating electrical cords and wires? Get him a friend. They keep each other busy.

- You might think that a kitten's playful stalking and attacking of your ankles or biting your hand is cute and endearing. But when that kitten becomes an adult who has not learned what is acceptable because he did not have another kitty companion, it's not fun anymore. Kittens teach each other important skills like bite inhibition and appropriate play.

- Kittens keep you up all night! Want your kitten to stop attacking your feet in bed while you're trying to sleep, running all over the place, and making a ruckus? Get him a friend. They'll play together until they're so tired they'll fall right asleep.

- If you think you might want two cats someday, why not adopt two now that already know and love each other so that you can save yourself the stress of introducing two unrelated adult cats later on?

- You're saving two lives instead of one!

Now that I've talked your ear off about the importance of having two kittens, what about if you're planning on adopting an adult cat? Should you still get two? The answer is probably not at the same time. With adult cats, it's best to adopt one, give him a chance to settle in first, and then go back for another one. You can also consider a bonded pair of adults – this is a pair of cats that already love each other very much and don't want to be separated. Although there are exceptions, most cats will generally enjoy the company of another cat. Be sure to ask the rescue or shelter if your cat has experience living with cats in the past or if they think the cat might enjoy it in the future. Advice for introducing cats to each other, as well as other pets and kids, will be outlined in another chapter.

Indoor, Outdoor, or Indoor/Outdoor?

Opinions can be strong when it comes to this topic. There are the people who have always had outdoor cats, and "they were just fine." And there are the people who are absolutely adamant that their cat will never be allowed outside, ever. I'm somewhere in between. I think that the safest place for the majority of cats is inside, but that the outdoors can be introduced appropriately.

There are a lot of arguments against outdoor cats:

- Risk of being hit by a car

- Risk of being attacked by a dog, fox, hawk, or other animal

- Risk of poison, disease, fleas/ticks/worms

- Risk of abuse by humans
- Risk of becoming lost, taken to a shelter, or kept by a well-meaning person
- Non-native predators cause devastation to the bird population

Photo Courtesy of Liora Engel-Smith

There are also a lot of arguments against strictly indoor cats:

- Boredom

- Obesity

- Destructive behavior

- Increased need to clean the litter box

- Increased pet dander and hair in the home

These downfalls of having a strictly indoor cat certainly do exist. Imagine being stuck inside your house 24/7, never leaving, and never being exposed to the outside world. It would probably drive you crazy, right? There's less room to exercise, you might start to act out, and you'd be bored out of your mind. However, I don't think that's an excuse to let cats out to free-roam and think that will solve all of these problems. According to a 2017 article in Catster, the lifespan of an indoor cat is about 15.1 years, whereas outdoor cats only live 5.625 years on average due to exposure to hazards.

There are exceptions as well. Many shelters adopt out "working cats" or "barn cats" as strictly outdoor, mouser-type cats, not pets. These cats normally have some type of severe behavioral problem that prevents them from being traditional indoor pets. Often, this working cat adoption is the last chance and only option for placement for the cat. If you have a warehouse, barn, garage, or other safe outdoor structure and would like an outdoor cat for pest control, consider inquiring about adopting a cat who needs this type of environment to be successful.

Indoor-only cats should be provided with plenty of daily enrichment, including "bringing the outdoors in!" There are many ways to safely exposure your indoor cat to the outside world.

- Cat grass, sold in most pet stores, is safe for kitties to chew on and even eat. You can even grow it yourself!

- Something as simple as opening your window and letting the fresh air in for a few minutes every day can be extremely enriching for cats. Have you ever noticed that the second you crack your window open, your cats come running? Even if it's chilly out, they'll enjoy a breath of fresh air once in a while.

- Training your cat to go outside on a harness and leash can also be fun and exciting for both of you. Be sure to very slowly get your cat used to the harness by putting it on him for a few minutes every day. Only once he is completely comfortable wearing a harness should you take him outside. He may be nervous outdoors at first, so remember to be patient and gradually introduce him.

- Many cat owners are hopping on the "catio" trend. Catios are outdoor enclosures so that your kitty can feel the fresh air and maybe a little grass on his paws, but in a way that he's protected from predators and prevented from getting lost. I converted my front porch into one, and my kitties love to sit and watch the birds from safely behind a screen.

- Place a bird feeder right outside a window and give cats a comfy place to perch beside it. Free Cat TV!

- Overall, it's at your discretion whether you prefer to keep your cat indoors or decide to let him outside from time to time. However, being primarily indoors with controlled and supervised exposure to the outdoors seems to work best to keep your kitty safe and healthy. Many

Photo Courtesy of Michael Mannschreck

rescues and shelters have indoor-only clauses in their adoption contracts simply because it's the safest option for your adopted cat. If you must let your cat outdoors, be sure that he wears a breakaway collar and tags and is microchipped so that he can be returned to you if he gets lost. Studies have shown that only about 1 to 5 percent of lost cats who enter shelters are returned to their owners, and this is primarily due to lack of identification.

Considering "Different" or "Special Needs" Cats

One day at my job at an animal shelter, I was speaking to a potential adopter who was looking at cats. I asked him what kind of cat he was looking for, and he said one who was young, friendly, and playful. I decided to show him Zeus, a 1-year-old brown tabby who had been witnessed being hit by a car before being brought to the shelter by a Good Samaritan. No owner came forward, and after a leg amputation, Zeus was as good as new – just one leg short. "Oh no, I'm an animal lover," the man said. "That makes me too sad."

That was the most confused I've ever felt. Zeus's story was sad, sure, but most shelter cats don't have a happy background. And he fit all the requirements the man had listed! I think it was the adopter's "polite" way of turning the cat down for looking a little different or being less than perfect. And it's true – cats who are considered special needs do have a harder time getting adopted than those who aren't. You often hear that black cats are statistically less likely to get adopted due to their color, and although it's great that people recognize that and make a conscious effort to adopt black cats, other "different" types of cats still aren't getting the publicity they deserve.

Senior cats, cats with missing eyes or limbs, cats with medical issues, FIV+ or FELV+ cats, deaf or blind cats – they all tend to sit a little bit longer in a shelter cage. Even the most beautiful cat who is fearful or shy and hiding in the back of its cage won't get noticed, either. When you go to meet potential new kitties, take time to meet the ones that don't stick out to you at first. If they have medical issues that you might consider a red flag but meet all your other requirements, ask a staff member or volunteer for more information. You may think FIV sounds scary at first, for example, but most FIV+ cats live normal, symptom-free lives. Ask to hear the fearful senior cat's story. How long has he been hiding back there? Why did he end up here? You may be surprised to hear the volunteer say that he is the sweetest cat in the world outside of a cage, but that environment just makes him nervous.

In my life, I've had all kinds of special needs cats: seniors, tripods, missing eyes, irritable bowel syndrome, neurologic issues, hyperthyroidism, tumors, and more. And I loved them all! Often, "special needs" doesn't even have to mean extra care or extra vet bills. Ask to meet the cats that don't stick out to you at first and research their condition, whether it's a behavioral or medical concern that's making them "less adoptable." You may be surprised what you end up taking home!

The Facts about Declawing

Declawing is something that many cat owners think about post-adoption as a quick and easy fix to keeping their cat from scratching. Maybe you have young children, or someone in the home is immunocompromised and cannot afford to have a cat scratch. Or you want to protect a new couch or carpet from falling victim to your cat's nails. These people may not be aware of what declawing actually entails.

To put it simply, declawing is much more than a simple nail trim. It's an amputation equivalent to removing your fingertips at the first joint. Whether it's done by laser, blade, or nail clipper, declawing forces cats to walk unnaturally on their toe tips, causing pain and early-onset arthritis, depression and irritability, and litter box issues. Cats who are declawed are also more likely to bite as they no longer have claws as a defense mechanism. In many cases, there can be regrowth of claws under the skin, causing severe pain and requiring additional corrective surgery. Tendonectomy surgeries also have high complication risks and require nail trims at least once a week for life.

Many countries have already outlawed this procedure, as well as several cities and states in the United States. The Humane Society of the United States opposes declawing except for very rare cases where it is medically necessary, like a tumor in the nail bed. The Center for Disease Control, the US Public Health Service, the National Institutes of Health, and infectious diseases experts also oppose declawing cats, as declawed cats are more likely to bite, which poses more of a risk to sick humans. I also personally strongly oppose declawing. There is ample evidence that declawed cats are more likely to end up in shelters due to medical or behavioral problems, which inevitably leads to increased euthanasia of declawed cats because the shelters are unable to adopt them out.

Should you adopt a cat who has already been declawed? Absolutely, yes. Inform yourself of the potential issues that may arise in the cat in the future, or perhaps may be the reason that the cat ended up in the shelter in the first place. The Paw Project, a nonprofit organization dedicated to ending the practice, recommends vets in each state that are informed in evaluating pain in declawed cats. If your declawed cat has litter box aversion or aggression concerns, speak to a veterinarian or certified cat behavior consultant for help keeping him as happy and healthy as possible.

Remember that scratching is a natural behavior in cats. Cats scratch to mark territory and secrete pheromones, stretch their muscles, and file their nails. Cats enjoy scratching. Taking the ability to scratch away from them takes away one of their great joys in life. Nail trimming or Soft Paws nail caps can make a big difference in keeping any damage to a minimum. Both are considered humane alternatives to declawing your cat. We'll cover how to redirect cats to appropriate scratching places and how to train your cat to accept nail trims later on in the book, too.

The Benefits of Spay/Neuter

If you adopt from a shelter or rescue, more than likely, your cat or kitten will already come spayed or neutered. In some cases, you may be given a voucher or coupon if your kitten is too young, or you may have to pay a deposit that will be returned to you after the surgery is completed. However, if you find an unaltered cat from a private owner who is rehoming, spay and neuter is a decision you'll need to put some thought into.

Obviously, the main benefit of spaying and neutering is that your cat can no longer reproduce. According to the American Society for the Prevention of Cruelty to Animals (ASPCA), approximately 1.5 million shelter animals are euthanized annually in the United States, including 860,000 cats. Although things are getting better, there are still many more cats in the United States than there are homes. Trust me; I know kittens are cute. I get that. But we just don't need any more. If you want the joy of raising kittens, try being a foster parent for a rescue or shelter! But don't let your own cat contribute to the overpopulation problem.

The following are myths about spay/neuter:

- My cat needs to have at least one heat cycle/one litter before I spay her. This is not based on fact and stems from the idea that your cat should be allowed to experience motherhood or that your children should be able to witness the "miracle of birth." In fact, spaying female cats before their first heat cycle greatly reduces their risk of developing mammary cancer and completely eliminates the risk of uterine or ovarian cancer. The more times a cat goes through a heat cycle, the more likely it

*Photo Courtesy
of Sampradha Gopalakrishnan*

is to develop a deadly uterine infection called pyometra. Pyometra is life-threatening, requires immediate emergency surgery, and will affect 25 percent of unaltered female cats at some point.

- My cat's personality will change after they are spayed/neutered. Yes, but not in the way you might think. Have you ever been around a female cat in heat? I don't recommend it. They scream constantly, try to escape out the front door, and yes – they flaunt what they have. Unaltered male cats are more likely to spray urine indoors to mark that they are available and may also try to escape and roam the neighborhood looking for females or fighting other male cats. Spaying and neutering eliminate these undesirable behaviors. In addition, altering a cat does not inherently make them fat or lazy – boredom and overfeeding will.

- I can't afford to get my cat fixed. More and more free and low-cost clinics are popping up across the United States. At the shelter where I work, it's only $40 to have your male cat neutered and vaccinated. PetSmart Charities has developed a search engine to help you find a low-cost clinic in your area. If you're still concerned about the cost, consider visiting a shelter that includes the cost of spay/neuter in your adoption fee. Most do! As a bonus, cities that require pet licensing usually charge you less if your pet is altered.

In summary, having your pet spayed or neutered is a no-brainer. It prevents costly medical issues and solves many behavior issues associated with having an intact cat. It also helps prevent pet overpopulation and euthanasia in shelters. It's a must-do for any cat!

ADVICE FROM THE EXPERTS

When potential adopters come to your rescue/shelter, what are your top tips for choosing the right cat for their lifestyle or family?

Usually people know whether they want a kitten or an adult cat. When adopting a kitten, we remind them a kitten plays endlessly, can keep you up at night, and needs constant human affection to teach it to be trusting and loving. Very young children need to be watched carefully and taught how to interact, or there could be scratching and biting. An older cat is much easier and can be left alone more than a kitten, but still needs human contact. Never walk past your cat without giving it a pet."

JUDE EPSTEIN
Much Love Animal Rescue

The first thing I do when an adopter visits our shelter is to try to assess the lifestyle of the adopting family or individual. Will the cat be living in a home with an older retired individual or couple? If that is the case, usually a middle-aged cat with a laid-back, passive personality would be best. Are there children in the family? Younger cats and most kittens over a few months old generally enjoy a more active environment. Younger cats thrive on playing games, chasing toys, and interacting with children. Depending on the environment that a cat lived in before being relinquished to our shelter, a combination of an indoor/outdoor environment may be best."

LARRY KACMARCIK
Blue Moon Cat Sanctuary

Don't be set on color or age. Use the guidance of our volunteers who know their foster cats' personalities, their likes and dislikes, their energy levels, and what types of environment would be best for particular cats. Let them help match you up with a great fit. The right fit makes for the best experience with your new pet."

KATIE JOHNSON
Actually Rescuing Cats

Look for a cat that engages with you. If you have other cats at home, are they male or female? Try to get the opposite sex. Are you looking for a young, energetic cat or one that is older, more relaxed, and settled? If you don't have another cat at home, have you thought about the amount of time you have to engage with a new cat, or would it be better to adopt two so they have each other?"

LYNDA STREEPER
Humane Society of Northern Virginia

I think the most important thing for potential adopters is to keep an open mind when they are looking for a 'furever' friend! Many potential adopters come in with an idea in their head of what they will take home, like a very young kitten that's a certain color with a long, fluffy coat. Some of my favorite adoption matches have been families that got 'chosen' by cats a little older and different from what they were initially looking for."

ELIZABETH FUDGE
Companion Animal Alliance

When potential adopters come to our rescue looking for the perfect new kitty family member, I think it's important for them to know what kind of personality they are looking for. Do they want a cat/kitten that's going to be a great fit for their other animals or kids? Do they want someone to cuddle and love on? It's really important to know what you're looking for in order to find the perfect cat, and it really helps me play matchmaker when deciding if a cat will be happy and loved in its forever home."

KATIE RIDLINGTON
AK Cat and Dog Rescue

It is all about the personality of the cat and the make-up of the family. Things to consider: other cats, dogs, kids, household energy level, etc. Some cats are 'I'm the king of the jungle and this is my jungle' type cats, meaning they want to be the one and only. Elderly cats typically don't want to be in a crazy, high-energy household; they prefer a snoozy type of place. Kittens need another cat friend or someone willing to play, play, play! Know the personality of your home first, and then think about your ideal kitty."

LINDA DIAMOND
SoBe Cats Spay & Neuter, Inc.

❝❝ *Talk to the foster parent(s) to really get to know the personality of the cat(s)/kitten(s) you are considering. Be honest about how much time and activity you can devote to a new pet. If you want a cat to cuddle and sit in your lap, consider an older cat that is less active. If you are very active or have kids who are, a younger kitten may be a great fit! Always keep in mind that kittens, especially, do better in pairs or groups. They learn from each other, entertain each other, and provide companionship when you are not available. If you have room for a pair (or more), it is a win-win. Also, keep in mind that kittens, just like babies, have not yet developed or expressed their complete personalities. If you want very specific character traits, an older kitten or an adult cat is a better option. Don't just pick a cat or kitten based on appearance. Make sure to meet the cat. In many cases, adopters feel an almost immediate bond when they find the right cat. I have seen fearful cats that were timid around everyone crawl into the arms of their perfect person and curl up against someone's chest with no hesitation. Everyone feels it when it is meant to be."*

CORI LYNN STANLEY
Averting CAT-astrophe

❝❝ *I encourage the adopters to look past the physical aspects of the cat or kitten and find a kitten who fits their lifestyle."*

MELISSA CHRISTMAN
San Antonio Feral Cat Coalition

❝❝ *The right cat has to have the same energy level as the home. If there are children and lots of activity, you need a kitty that is confident and outgoing. If it's a quiet home, a calm and relaxed cat is the best fit."*

MARILEE WELLS
Maricats Rescue

CHAPTER 2

Rescue vs. Shelter vs. Private Owner: How Do I Choose?

Most people know they want to adopt or rescue a cat but may become overwhelmed by all their options. I opened Petfinder.com and did a search, and there were 5,500 cats available for adoption within 100 miles of my house! And according to Petfinder again, there are...wait for it...roughly 160 different shelter or rescue groups in my state, Maryland, that all have pets listed for adoption. In total, Petfinder has nearly 14,000 shelters and rescues across the United States that use their website to post animals for adoption. All of these shelters and rescues have different processes. Some have physical locations, whereas for others, you'll be meeting your cat inside a foster home. I want to start out by outlining the difference between shelters and rescues and explaining how and why they do things.

Photo Courtesy of Michele Fellows

Shelters

Shelters are physical buildings that house cats, and usually dogs and other animals, for adoption. There are two main types: municipal, government-run, open-admission shelters; and private, usually limited-admission shelters. I'll refer to them from now on as either open- or limited-admission shelters. **Under no circumstances should you ever use the terms "kill-shelter" or "no-kill shelter" or use these determinations to decide where to adopt or give your support.** These outdated, inaccurate terms do nothing other than turn the public against shelters doing their best.

Limited-admission shelters, or what I have instructed you not to call "no-kill" shelters, are commonly run by a private organization. They accept owner surrenders and may take in animals from partner shelters in the area or around the nation, but they usually do not take in strays. The biggest difference between these shelters and open-admission comes with the word "limited." They have limited intake, only accept animals that meet their standards for health and behavior, and do not take in any more animals than they can handle. This means that if they meet maximum capacity for cats, and someone walks in looking to surrender their cat, they would turn them away.

This is how these shelters avoid high euthanasia rates – they never have to euthanize animals simply because there is not enough room for them because they can say no whenever they want. Limited-admission shelters do euthanize animals for health and behavior reasons, and no shelter is exempt from those difficult decisions.

Open-admission shelters, in contrast, have to take in any animal that walks through their doors. It doesn't matter if they're at capacity. If it's a busy summer with a lot of owner surrenders, and every cage is already full, and suddenly they receive a hoarding case of 92 cats through animal control – they gotta make room somehow. This is where they receive the "kill-shelter" label. It means that sometimes they are faced with making the horrible decision of what animal gets to stay and who has to go.

Luckily, euthanasia rates are steadily dropping as more people become involved in animal welfare and dedicate their time and money towards making a change. A decade ago, those 92 cats coming in from a hoarding case would've meant 92 other cats not making it out of the shelter alive. Now, shelters are lowering their intake rates through education and admissions deferment strategies, spay and neuter programs, better adoption programs, better return-to-owner rates for pets brought in stray, and partnerships with rescue groups to get at-risk animals out of the shelter quickly to make room

*Photo Courtesy
of Julie Ricketts*

for new ones coming in. According to the ASPCA, 1.5 million shelter animals are euthanized annually in the United States, which is a huge drop from approximately 2.6 million in 2011.

The public should support both types of shelters, but open-admission shelters need you the most. They are still suffering the consequences of the antiquated "kill-shelter" terminology and have the least resources. The live-release rate, or percentage of live outcomes for animals, at your local shelter is public information and easily accessed. Over 90 percent affords the shelter a "no-kill" designation, and you'll find that many open-admission shelters are able to meet that designation despite their increased challenges. If you are angry about the euthanasia rate at your local shelter, the best thing to do is volunteer, donate, foster, or adopt, and you'll be helping them to save lives.

Rescues

Rescue groups are often confused with shelters. The big difference is that shelters have a physical building where they house animals, and usually, rescue groups are private and completely volunteer-run. All or most of their animals are in private foster homes. Often, rescues and shelters maintain good relationships with each other and help each other out when possible. Shelters normally obtain their animals either from pet owners who can no longer keep their pets or from taking in pets that have been found stray in the community. Some shelters work with their local animal control and might take in cruelty and neglect cases as well.

Rescues, on the other hand, usually don't take owner surrenders, and if they do, it's on a limited, case-by-case basis. Rescues do not have the legal authority to take in stray pets (in most cases) and cannot assist with any concerns of cruelty or neglect you see in your community. They primarily pull at-risk animals from overcrowded shelters and get them out of that stressful environment and into a comfortable foster home. Animals at risk could mean many things depending on the shelter and its current situation. It could be a senior cat who has been overlooked because he is scared in a cage or a dog that needs extra training in order to be successful in a home. It could be a litter of kittens that need to be bottle-fed and given round-the-clock care. Due to their unique needs, these animals are best helped in the home of a foster family rather than a kennel environment. I'll talk more about fostering pets in another chapter.

FUN FACT

ASPCA Shelter Finder

The American Society for the Prevention of Cruelty to Animals or ASPCA is headquartered in New York City and is one of the largest humane societies in the world. The ASPCA operates specialized shelter programs in New York, Los Angeles, and North Carolina. If you're looking for a shelter outside of these regions, you can use the ASPCA website to locate cats in your local shelter. For more information, visit aspca.org.

There are advantages and disadvantages to adopting from shelters and rescues. Here's a pros and cons list for each to help you decide which route to adoption works best:

ADOPTING FROM A SHELTER	
Pros	**Cons**
Shelters give you the ability to view many animals for adoption at the same time. There are many cats in one building rather than spread out across many foster homes.	Some animals in the shelter may have no known history whatsoever. If the cat you like came in as a stray, there's no way of knowing if he gets along with dogs, for example, before you bring him home.
Shelters usually allow same-day adoptions. You can walk in, choose a cat, and bring the cat home within a few hours.	Shelters can be a very stressful and frightening place for a cat to be. You may not see their true personality in a shelter cage if they are very scared or stressed.
Many shelters practice an "Adopters Welcome" mentality, meaning that there are fewer barriers and hoops to jump through. The goal of this policy is to encourage more people to adopt by making it an easy and non-judgmental process.	
Generally, adoption fees are lower in shelters than in rescues.	

ADOPTING FROM A RESCUE GROUP

Pros	Cons
You will be able to meet the cat in a more natural environment and see what it's like when it is relaxed and at home. What you see in the foster home is much closer to what you'll get in your own home.	Because you're going to a person's home to meet your cat, you'll only be able to meet one at a time. If you don't fall in love with the first cat, you'll have to start the process over again.
Your cat's foster parent will know all about the cat because they've lived with him! You can have all your questions answered before making a decision.	The adoption process through a rescue can take days or weeks. They also may have stricter requirements for adoption than shelters.
Rescues are smaller and volunteer-run, so they rely on adoption fees to keep being able to save lives. You'll be able to feel good knowing that your fee went directly towards saving another cat.	Generally, adoption fees are higher in rescues than in shelters. This is because they do not receive any government funding, and usually, adoption fees and donations are their only source of income.

I have personally adopted from both types of organizations, and I honestly don't prefer one over the other. Both have cats for adoption that really need good homes. It really comes down to what's important to you: Do you want to know every little detail about your new kitty before you bring him home? Or do you want the ability to look at a lot of cats before you settle on one? Can you wait a week or so to go through an adoption process, or do you want to go home with a cat today? Either type is a great option for saving a life. In both cases, you actually get to save two lives: the cat you adopted and the cat that space has now opened up for in the shelter or rescue.

Why Do I Need to Pay an Adoption Fee?
AKA the Myth of the "Free Kitten"

You meet the kitten of your dreams in her foster home. Everything is perfect, you've picked out all her supplies, and you're ready to bring her home. All that's left is to pay the adoption fee. But you're doing a good deed by saving a life! And now the rescue expects you to give them $100 on top of everything? Why?

Believe it or not, I get this question a lot. Adoption fees can be expensive, and I totally understand wanting to know why. Expect to spend anywhere

Photo Courtesy
of Sampradha Gopalakrishnan

from $0 - $150 in adoption fees for a cat or kitten. However, in reality, that healthy, rambunctious little 8-week-old kitten cost the rescue a lot more than $100. According to the Humane Society of the United States, 80 percent of kittens are born outdoors to feral cats. So, your kitten likely was scooped up from somewhere outdoors. Maybe his mother was hit by a car, and he needed to be bottle-fed to survive. Maybe he was undersocialized from not being exposed to people for the first couple weeks of his life, and her foster had to spend time getting him to adjust to humans. Not only did this take time and dedication from a volunteer, it also cost money to feed and care for the kitten. Then there are the other expenses to get cats ready to go home[1]:

- Flea treatment: $12

- Dewormer: $10

- Microchip: $25

- FIV/FELV combo test: $45

- Rabies vaccine: $16

- FVRCP vaccines (3 total): $75

- Spay/neuter: $100

Photo Courtesy of Jenna Martin

That comes to $283 per kitten, $183 more than your $100 adoption fee. This doesn't include if your kitten was sick with an upper respiratory infection, conjunctivitis, ringworm, earmites, intestinal parasites, or one of the other very common illnesses found in kittens born outside. Rescues don't make any money off adoption fees and don't turn a profit. This also means that the "free kitten" you picked up off the side of the road, in reality, will cost you a lot more than one adopted from a rescue! Rescues rely completely on donations to keep running, and your adoption

1 Pricing from Jarrettsville Veterinary Center - https://jarrettsvillevet.com/

fee will always be cycled back to help take care of medical bills for the next animal in need. Rest assured that the adoption fee is going to a great cause, and your new kitty will be worth every penny!

Why Do I Need to Complete an Application?

Adoption applications can be daunting. Every rescue or shelter will have its own to fill out. If you are shopping around and looking at multiple cats in multiple places, it can get time-consuming and tiresome.

Rescues are private organizations, meaning they can set their own processes and usually have more strict adoption guidelines. They may ask for references and call your landlord. They may ask for proof that any current

Photo Courtesy of Cassie O'Dell

pets in the home are neutered and vaccinated or even do a home visit. Many adopters can be turned off by being put under so much scrutiny. It is important to note that these rescues only have the pet's best interest in mind. They want to be absolutely positive that the next family this cat goes to is their forever family, and he will never be abused or neglected

FUN FACT

How Many Cats Come from Shelters?

According to the ASPCA, around 2.1 million cats were adopted from shelters in 2019 in the United States. Cats make up about half of the animals adopted from shelters each year.

again. However, I totally understand the frustration that may come with such an in-depth evaluation or even a rejection. I have been denied by a rescue before, myself!

My advice is if you are denied, if you don't get a response, or if the process is just too much, move on. Consider visiting a shelter instead or searching for a rescue that is willing to have a conversation with you instead. For example, I have worked with rescues that ask your opinion of declawing cats on their application. If you answer that you've always had declawed cats and you plan to do the same for your new kitten, you will almost certainly be denied. This approach does not allow for the education of the potential adopter. Maybe you have never been told the facts about declawing cats, and it was just what you thought everyone did. That person who is denied without reason will apply over and over and continue to become more and more frustrated until they pick up a free kitten on Craigslist and have it declawed anyway. Do you see the problem?

We talked a little bit earlier about the "Adopters Welcome" movement and how it can often be a shorter and simpler process to adopt from a shelter. Adopters Welcome was a research project by the Humane Society of the United States. It found that removing barriers to adoption and having conversations with adopters instead of having them complete a strict application process increased the number of adoptions and actually kept more pets in homes.

I highly recommend asking the shelter or rescue you're thinking of working with if they practice these values in their adoption process. You might also ask your friends or neighbors for recommendations as to where they went to rescue their cat. Regardless, if you're frustrated, please continue pressing on. By reading this book, you're already a more educated adopter and the type of person who would be a great cat owner. You'll find your perfect kitty!

ADVICE FROM THE EXPERTS

Should a new owner choose to adopt through a rescue or an animal shelter? What are the pros and cons of each, and what should go into the decision?

Any animal coming from a rescue has the advantage of being fostered, which allows for a complete health, personality, and behavior assessment. There are no disadvantages to adopting from a rescue. Shelters often have staff that will get to know a particular animal, so can tell the adopters something about the cat, but having never seen the animal in a home, there are a lot of factors they won't know. There are also health risks coming from a shelter, and any new adoptee should be taken immediately to a vet."

JUDE EPSTEIN
Much Love Animal Rescue

Rescues like ours get to know the cat, its health issues, and its personality. Unfortunately, we can't typically afford treatment for complicated health issues like teeth problems. Animal shelters generally have a veterinarian on staff that can treat any health issue, but the quantity of animals they get limits their ability to learn each cat's personality."

ANNA SEALS
Central Indiana Foster Cats

In a lot of ways they are similar, it really depends on the kind of cat you're looking for and its personality. A rescue will usually have a more intimate knowledge of the cat than a shelter since we spend significantly more time with individual animals, but shelters will have more options since their turn¬over is usually quicker."

MELISSA SHELTON
Forget-Me-Not Barn Cats

CONTINUE

" *The benefit of adopting through a rescue is that the majority house their cats in foster homes. So foster families are able to learn their personalities a lot more than an animal shelter could. For example, foster families will be able to tell potential adopters if a cat is good with children or other animals. Animal shelters just won't have that kind of information. That being said, either option is wonderful!"*

LESLIE THOMAS
Itty Bitty Kitty Committee

" *When a new owner is trying to decide whether or not to adopt from a shelter or a rescue, there are a few factors to consider. If adopters are looking for a fast-paced adoption process, a shelter might be a better option. Rescues typically have rescued animals residing in the foster volunteers' homes, so it may take a little more time to connect with the foster volunteer, discuss the cat/kitten to see if it is a good match, and then set up a meet and greet that works for both the potential adopter and also the foster volunteer. When adopting from a shelter, as mentioned, the process is faster, and you have the ability to see all of the animals that the shelter has to offer in just one visit. It is also a humbling and joyful feeling to save an animal from a sometimes sterile shelter environment. Alternatively, when adopting from a rescue, the benefits are that adopters are able to discuss, in depth, the personality, demeanor, and history of the animal with the foster volunteer who has actually worked with and cared for the cat or kitten on a regular basis. You receive quite a bit more detailed information, thus ultimately helping adopters to make the correct decisions about adopting. Adopting from shelters can be impulsive, whereas adopting from rescues gives time for pause and consideration."*

MICHELLE BASS
A Kitten Place, Inc.

" *Rescues live with the animals they adopt and can therefore tell adopters exactly what personality they are getting. Each animal adopted from a rescue helps to open space for a rescue to pull from a local shelter (if they have that program). A shelter does not truly know the animal's personality outside of a cage."*

JULIA MELTON
Summit Animal Rescue Assn.

> *There are many advantages to adopting through a rescue. In most cases, the animals will be completely vetted, including all age-appropriate vaccinations and spay/neuter. Some shelters require adopters to return to complete vetting. Additionally, foster families learn a lot about the personalities of their foster pets. The foster family can tell you if the cat gets along with dogs or is afraid of them. They will know if the cat is kid friendly or if it gets along with other cats. They can tell you the little things, like if the cat likes pâté but not shredded wet food or is afraid of ceiling fans! Rescues also adopt out kitties with special needs. Cats with one eye or three legs get a chance through a rescue that shelters rarely provide. If you want a cat that is unique and special and in some cases don't mind providing a little extra care, a rescue will give you options that a shelter cannot. Rescue foster parents are deeply invested in their foster kitties. Rescue parents are always happy to answer questions after adoption. If your kitty has an upset tummy from the stress of a new home, the foster parent will be happy to provide helpful advice like, 'I added baby rice cereal to her wet food right after I got her to help with her upset tummy when I first brought her home.' With all this in mind, rescue adoption fees may be slightly higher than shelter adoption fees. Rescue groups will also have much stricter application requirements than shelters do, like not allowing declawing or not allowing the pet to roam free outdoors. Both rescues and shelters will take a kitty back into their care if the match doesn't work out."*

CORI LYNN STANLEY
Averting CAT-astrophe

> *Rescues and shelters both serve equally important purposes. Often, a rescue is able to give more specific details on how a cat will behave in a home; rescues are able to test the cat with other animals, children, adults, strangers, etc. A cat in a shelter may behave in a drastically different manner than a cat in a home (so don't judge a shy shelter cat for its nervous behavior!). The downfall of a rescue is that we don't have an adoption floor as all of our cats are in foster homes, so you can't meet all of the cats and then make a decision on which one to adopt; you have to rely on pictures and videos before you fill out an application. In addition, rescues often are all volunteer, so if you are looking to adopt a cat on a spur-of-the-moment decision, you will need to wait for the rescue to approve your application and schedule a time to meet the cat at a foster home."*

MICAIAH ROY
Community Cat Advocates Inc.

> " Each offer many wonderful pets looking for homes. Depending on the area the shelter supports, it may not have funding for veterinary care like spay/neuter, or shots besides rabies or testing for FIV and FeLV; shelters usually have very little information on the cat, but the adoption fee is usually lower. A rescue spends the money and vets the cat, running tests and ensuring it's spay or neutered before going to its new home. Rescues typically have more time to spend with the cat to get a better idea of personality, play levels, and socialization. Typically you can bring your current pet to either place to test with the new one, but you risk exposure to more illness at a shelter than a rescue. Either is a good place to adopt from because it frees up a spot for another homeless or displaced pet."

LYNDA STREEPER
Humane Society of Northern Virginia

> " Either option is fine! So long as a cat in need has found a loving family, it really doesn't matter if it was a shelter or rescue group who placed the cat. Shelter cats can have more health problems and behavior issues because they are in a cage or environment with many other cats. But the positive for cats from a shelter is they have been around dogs, so families with dogs in the home or who are going to add a dog to the family may be a great option to see how a cat is with a dog. Rescue cats are typically foster-based in a family setting with fewer cats and stresses."

CHERYL MCMURRAY
Nile Valley Egyptian Foundation Inc.

CHAPTER 3

The Two Sides of Rehoming

On occasion, rather than us going to look for a new cat, the cat finds us instead. According to the ASPCA, only 31 percent of pet cats in the United States were obtained from a shelter or rescue. Where the heck do the other 69 percent come from? Around 27 percent were found as strays. Only 3 percent were acquired from a breeder, and the rest of them came from friends or family, private owners, or "other." Let's talk about all the other possible paths you may end up taking to bring a new kitty home.

What to Do if You've Found a Stray Cat or Kittens

Where I live in Baltimore, you can't turn a corner without seeing an outdoor cat or two or three. I have found several over the years just in my own front yard! It's no wonder that it's so common to see people adopting cats they've found as strays.

Photo Courtesy of Keith Lynch

It's important to explain the difference between a stray cat and a true outdoor or feral cat. When I say "stray," I mean a cat who formerly lived indoors and has either been lost or intentionally left outside by its owner. When identifying if a cat is stray, you can look at the following:

• **Is the cat clean or unkempt and dirty?** Most people assume dirty cats are outdoor or feral cats. It's actually the opposite! Cats who live outside are

Photo Courtesy
of Summer Spain

savvy and street smart and know how to stay sparkling clean even in a filthy environment. A cat who has been lost or dumped will not know how to care for itself outside, so it may be dirty, skinny, matted, or sickly looking. Generally, true outdoor cats can take proper care of themselves.

- **Is the cat trying to get indoors?** An outdoor cat is happy outside, whether it's sunny and warm or snowy and frigid. Conversely, cats who are used to living indoors will often try to get back inside where they are used to living.

- **Is the cat ear tipped?** When a cat has gone through a trap, neuter, return (TNR) program with the intention of releasing the cat back outside, vets will cut the tip of the feline's left ear to indicate that it has been fixed. If the kitty you find is missing a little bit of his ear, chances are, he's where he belongs. This is not 100 percent accurate as you do on occasion see indoor cats who have been ear-tipped, but it's a good place to start.

- **Can the cat be safely handled?** This is perhaps the most obvious indicator, but a cat who has been lost or abandoned is typically used to human interaction and may approach you on his own. A cat who lives outdoors will be skittish and avoid you, so it probably won't make the best house guest. A friendly cat will also be more likely to meow and carry its tail high in the air, indicating social behavior and a willingness to be approached. Cats who are lost may hunker down in one place and not move, exhibiting the "freeze" behavior from fight, flight, or freeze because they are afraid of their unfamiliar surroundings.

FUN FACT
Trap-Neuter-Return-Monitor

TNRM programs are considered a humane method for controlling stray cat populations in many areas around the world. TNRM includes capturing stray cats, vaccinating them against rabies, neutering them, and returning them to their community. The monitoring aspect of this method is usually undertaken by a local cat caretaker who can identify and trap new intact cats who join the community. By neutering stray cats in the community, the population of stray cats can gradually decrease, leaving more space, resources, and a healthier environment. According to the ASPCA, "Community Cats" are "unowned, free-roaming cats." When these cats end up in shelters, they are often euthanized because many of them are too feral to transition to living in a home. Thus, community cats are prime candidates for a TNRM program.

If the cat you've found is skittish or outwardly aggressive towards you, seems at ease in his environment, is well-kempt, and has an ear tip, leave him be. If you want to make his life a little easier, consider putting some food out for him and providing him with shelter, especially during cold weather. If he is not ear-tipped but meets the other criteria, get in touch with your local shelter or rescue group to help you trap the cat so he can be neutered and put back outside. Neutering him will keep him healthier and happier outdoors and prevent him from making kittens that will inevitably contribute to the overpopulation problem in animal shelters.

If the cat is friendly and trying to get inside, you have a different problem! Congratulations, you have a cat now! Well, not quite. Like I said earlier, these friendly stray cats might have been purposely abandoned, but it's also just as possible that they are someone's missing pet. Cats who are not used to surviving on their own can decline rapidly outdoors. Life is tough when you're not being served a bowl of kibble twice a day!

If you find a stray cat, the best thing to do is to bring him indoors and place him in your bathroom. Bathrooms are easily cleaned in case of fleas or disease or if you don't have a spare litter box! Keep the cat separated from kids and all other pets until he can be evaluated by a vet. Everyone can do this simple thing for just one night, even if your intentions are not to keep the cat. Animal control will not come out to pick up a cat who is not contained. If you can't safely get the cat inside your bathroom, TNR is best. Now you begin the process of trying to locate the owner if there is one.

Check with your local animal shelter to see what is required of you at this point. If they have a surrender law, you're required to turn the cat over to the shelter, usually within 24 hours of finding him. Even if they don't have a surrender law, it's almost always a good idea to turn the cat over unless you're fully committed to searching for an owner on your own before keeping the cat or responsibly finding him a new home. The shelter will be able to scan the cat for a microchip, which is a tiny chip the size of a grain of rice usually implanted between the cat's shoulder blades under the skin. Although the microchip does not contain a GPS tracker as some people think, it can be scanned and reveal the owner's information so that the cat can be quickly reunited with its family. Any veterinarian can also scan the cat for a microchip. Shelters are usually the first place that people who are missing their pets will check, too.

Finally, if the cat is sick or injured and is in need of medical care, shelters are equipped to handle that too. Some shelters will have "finder's holds" where you have the first right to adopt the cat after a holding period. The shelter will also spay or neuter, disease test, and vaccinate the cat. Be sure to contact your local shelter to find out what the laws are in your area. If you've done your due diligence and either completed the hold at the shelter or been unsuccessful in locating the owner on your own, then you are free to keep your new kitty! If you've found a stray kitty, but you don't want to keep him and would like to find him a new family on your own rather than surrender him to a shelter (after you've tried to look for the original owner, of course!), be sure to read the section on rehoming later on in this chapter.

ADVICE FROM THE EXPERTS

If someone finds a stray cat and wants to keep it, what advice would you give them before making that decision?

Always take the cat home, even if you decide to rehome it later. It is always best to save a life and bring a cat indoors. The cat might also be someone's lost pet—so you should take it to a vet to have it scanned for a microchip. It can take weeks or longer to get to know the true personality of a cat, so don't make a decision too quickly. A newly rescued cat is often shy and scared, but once it gets to know you, it will warm up, bond, and show its true personality. So always bring the cat inside, and take it to a vet to scan for a microchip and get basic medical care—flea treatment, deworming, FVRCP vaccine, FIV/FeLV test, and spay/neuter (if intact). If you take a cat home and decide to only foster until another home is found, it will be very easy to find a rescue group to help find the cat a new home as fosters are their biggest obstacle. They often can't 'take' the cat, but if you are fostering, the rescue will help find it a home. But give it some time and get to know the cat after it has warmed up, before deciding whether to keep or rehome."

AVARIE SHEVIN
Stray Cat Alliance

Before anyone wants to keep a stray cat they found, several steps should be taken first. It is always best to take the cat to a local vet and have it scanned for a microchip. It may have simply become lost or wandered away from its home. If an owner cannot be found, the cat should be examined thoroughly by a qualified veterinarian, spayed or neutered, tested for feline aids and feline leukemia, given a rabies shot, have all vaccinations updated, be treated for any fleas, and be examined for worms and ear mites."

LARRY KACMARCIK
Blue Moon Cat Sanctuary

First things first: take it to a vet! They can scan for a microchip to ensure that the cat isn't just lost. Also, it's very important to have the cat combo-tested, especially if you have other cats in your home! Combo testing will ensure that you don't take any communicable diseases back to your cats! Lastly, I would advise bringing the cat into one room only for a few days to decompress."

LESLIE THOMAS
Itty Bitty Kitty Committee

Not all outdoor cats are strays! We see this daily; a well-meaning person sees a cat on the doorstep and puts out food (which the cat eagerly takes advantage of). The person then assumes the cat was starving and clearly has no owner. In most cases, cats are opportunists and despite having food at home, they will gladly eat at every house in the neighborhood. We advise people to place a paper collar on the cat with a note asking if the cat has a home, along with a phone number. If, after several days, the cat is still wearing the collar, and no one has reached out, we advise that the finder take pictures and post them on social media (bonus points if you have a town or city group specific to you) to try to locate a possible owner. If these avenues are unsuccessful, we suggest bringing the cat to a vet or shelter to have it scanned for a microchip and a general physical (especially if the finder has other pets inside the home). A good rule of thumb is that if the cat looks well fed and groomed, it likely has a home."

MICAIAH ROY
Community Cat Advocates Inc.

If someone finds a cat (or the cat finds them!), and no owner can be found, adopting the cat can be very rewarding! If the adopter already has a cat in the home, it is of utmost importance to quarantine the new cat until it can be examined by a veterinarian and tested for FIV and FELV, two highly contagious diseases that come with serious health consequences and can result in death! We also inform the finder that adopting a cat is a 15- to 20-year commitment and sometimes more! The cat must be made comfortable with any changes the household experiences during that time, such as moving to a new home or the arrival of a new baby. The cat must be treated as and remain part of the family!"

ROSEMARY TOROK
Community Cat Companions

> *We often caution people about keeping a stray cat that they have found for a variety of reasons. The cat may belong to someone and may have wandered. It is always recommended that you take the animal to a local vet clinic to be scanned for a microchip to see if the cat was previously owned and can be returned to its rightful owner. Secondly, rescues and shelters have much better resources and abilities to get the cat the proper veterinary checkup and vaccinations, spay or neuter—usually at a much lower cost than an individual in the community would charge. People also need to be aware that they do not know the history of the cat and any diseases or infections it may have that might be transmittable to other pets."*

MICHELLE BASS
A Kitten Place, Inc.

> *First, go to a vet and have the cat scanned for a microchip. Most vets will do this for free, and it can lead to the owner. If the cat isn't chipped, contact the animal control for the county in which the cat was found so that if there are owners searching for the cat, they have a chance to find it. If your cat escaped, you would want that opportunity. If no owner comes forward, take the cat to the vet to determine if it is healthy so that you know what you are taking on before committing to the cat. You also want to be sure you have the time and ability to provide routine and emergency care when needed. Then you just want to make sure it's a good fit for your family, including any pets you already have."*

KIM KAY
Angels Among Us Pet Rescue

Obtaining a Cat from a Private Owner

The other main way people acquire cats is through rehoming, a direct transfer from a previous owner's home to a new owner's home. This could be from a friend, family member, neighbor, random person on social media, etc. There are several things you may want to know before bringing your new cat home. Feel free to ask some or all of the following questions:

Why are you rehoming? This is a must-ask. Maybe they are moving to a place where pets are not allowed, or the new baby is allergic. But perhaps they have a cat with litter box issues or aggression problems. Understandably, not every new cat owner is prepared to take on those challenges.

What is the cat's history? This question includes where they got the cat, how long they've had him, how many previous owners he's had, etc.

Are there other animals/ children in the home? If you have three dogs and four kids at home, and the cat has always been an only pet with an elderly couple, maybe it's not the best match. That type of cat is probably best suited for a quiet home and may have trouble adjusting to all the activity.

FUN FACT
Cat Rehoming Statistics

In 2019, the ASPCA estimated that around 100,000 cats who entered shelters in the United States were strays returned to their owners. In addition, according to the ASPCA National Rehoming Survey, 42% of cat owners rehomed their cats due to pet problems such as aggression, size, or unmanageable health problems.

How old is the cat? Is he spayed/neutered? When was he last at the vet? These are essential questions to ask. You get a picture of the cat's health and also an idea of how much you'll be spending at the vet yourself. Don't be afraid to ask if they can get the cat up to date on shots before rehoming. They may say no, but it doesn't hurt to ask!

What kind of food, litter box, toys, etc., does the cat like? Knowing his preferences will ease your cat's transition to a new place.

There are more questions you might have, but these are the essentials. Some owners may ask for updates or visitation rights, and this may or may not be something you're comfortable with, especially if the person is a stranger. It's okay to say no and move on. Cat owners may also have reasons for rehoming that you don't agree with or problems that you would approach differently. I just want to take a minute to talk about approaching these types of situations with kindness and trying to withhold judgment.

There is a story I've heard that always sticks with me about a man who was rehoming his 15-year-old cat on Craigslist. It was a simple post along the lines of, "I'm moving, and I can't bring my cat with me. It breaks my heart to do this, but I have to give her up. She is free to a good home." Your immediate thoughts, if they're anything like mine were, are angry and judgmental. How dare this man discard his senior cat like trash just because he was moving? Maybe you're thinking, "I would live in my car before I gave up my cat." People sent this man death threats. He received dozens of emails, all of

Photo Courtesy of Esther Adams

them cursing him out and calling him names. Finally, he received one email from a local rescue group with an offer to help.

This man had been diagnosed with a terminal illness. He had had his beautiful cat since she was a kitten and loved her with all of his heart. He was preparing to move into hospice care over the coming weeks, and although he begged, he was not allowed to take the cat with him. He wanted the best for her and was trying to do the right thing, but the messages he received made him feel even more guilty and in despair. The rescue fulfilled the man's dying wish and found his cat a wonderful forever home, passing on a life lesson to their followers to just be kind because you never know what people are going through.

I encourage you to keep this story in mind when seeing posts on social media of people rehoming their pets. Even in situations where people probably do deserve judgment, remember that kindness is always the most productive way to help the animal in need.

How to Identify a Scam/Red Flags

In 2017, the Better Business Bureau conducted a study that showed 12.5 percent of all reported online purchase fraud on Craigslist was related to puppy and kitten scams, with tens of thousands of consumers filing reports. Red flags for a scam are:

- Insisting that you pay the adoption/rehoming fee upfront before meeting the kitten in person
- Limited photos that may look like stock photos
- Asking for payment via Western Union or MoneyGram
- Offering popular purebred breeds like Persians, Sphynxes, or Bengals at a low price
- Ads with strange sentence structure or poor spelling/grammar

If you think you may be facing a scam, the safest thing to do is to insist on meeting the kitten in person before exchanging any money. If the "owner" is reluctant to allow you to do this, move on. You can absolutely find a furry friend on Craigslist or Facebook, but it's your responsibility to be careful and safe while doing so. If it sounds too good to be true, it probably is.

The Problem with Pet Shops

Not many pet shops sell animals anymore, thankfully, but there are still some out there. I'm not talking about stores like PetSmart, Petco, and Pet Supplies Plus that work with local rescues to house rescue cats for adoption. These stores are all great options to visit and meet your next best friend. I'm specifically discussing stores that support puppy and kitten mills and sell animals for a profit.

If you've never heard of puppy mills, they are commercial farming operations where purebred animals are raised in massive quantities, usually in substandard and inhumane conditions. Currently, there are hundreds of thousands of animals in puppy mills that will breed the puppies and kittens you find in pet stores. Not only do puppy and kitten mills contribute heavily

Photo Courtesy of Ali Johnson

to the pet overpopulation problem, but the animals are likely kept in cages for their entire lives and used as commodities rather than ever being cared for as members of the family. Instead of breeding for quality, with a focus on the health and temperament of the pets, puppy and kitten mills breed for quantity. The more kittens they can sell, the better.

The reality is, no responsible breeder would allow their kittens to be sold in a pet shop, where there is little education for or pre-screening of purchasers. Kittens for sale in pet stores are always sourced inhumanely, despite what the employees may tell you. Please adopt, don't shop. If you must have a purebred cat, choose a responsible, quality breeder and avoid pet shops that sell kittens at all costs.

Responsible Rehoming: When It Just Doesn't Work Out

No one ever adopts a cat or dog expecting that it won't work out. Most people have high expectations of a lifelong friend and companion and are prepared for the long haul. They never expect that life will get in the way, and they may have to make a difficult decision. I want to start out by saying that there are very few reasons I judge people for giving up a pet. Shaming owners that are trying to do the best for their animals is never okay. Just because you would do something differently doesn't mean that the owner is a bad person.

Working in a shelter, I have seen every reason imaginable for giving up a pet, from aggression to housebreaking issues, a new baby in the home or moving, the pet having fleas or its owner becoming homeless, the owner escaping domestic violence, or just plain not wanting a pet anymore. Sometimes, a little bit of education and help with pet food is all people need. Other times, you just want to grab the cat and tell it everything is going to be okay now that it's away from that person.

I often ask myself, "is the cat really better off with that person than they would be in a new home?" Do I really expect the person to keep a dog who has bitten three people? Do I expect the single mom who has just been evicted to keep her two cats in her car with her children? No, and it's not fair to treat them with anything other than empathy. I told the story of the old man on Craigslist earlier, and that should ring true in your mind every time you see someone posting their cat for adoption on social media. You never really know

Photo Courtesy
of Jennifer Cello

what a person is going through. Kindness helps both the cat and the person; judgment and shaming will help neither. Robin Williams said, "Everyone you meet is fighting a battle you know nothing about. Be kind. Always."

That being said, I want to talk about what should happen if you can no longer keep your cat. The reason doesn't matter to me. What I care about is that you're rehoming responsibly and in the best interest of the cat. The first thing to remember is that if you have adopted your cat from a shelter or a rescue, they will just about always accept the cat back. Many rescues have a line in their contract that says you must return the cat to them. You always have those options. The problem is if you didn't adopt your cat from a shelter or rescue and have to give him up. Now what?

- Update your cat's vaccinations and make sure he is neutered before listing him for rehoming. Ensuring that he is nice and healthy before he goes to his new home will make it easier on the new owner, and it will also make the cat more attractive when listing him for adoption.

- Take eye-catching photos and write an honest but appealing biography. Most people will skip right on by a post without a photo. Be sure your photo is high quality and shows your cat's good side. Consider dressing him up in a bow tie if he'll tolerate it, or at the minimum, make sure he is well-groomed. Things to include in your biography are age, spay/neuter status, the reason you're rehoming, if good with kids/cats/dogs, and any medical/behavior issues. And, of course, don't forget to include things that make your cat special. Does he know any tricks? Greet you at the front door? Have a favorite toy? You want to be honest but also show off your cat's best self, and set him apart from others.

- Consider listing your cat on AdoptaPet.com. They have a free rehoming service that will help you advertise and screen potential adopters! GetYourPet.com also has a similar service. Social media is a great place to advertise as well. You can also make good old-fashioned flyers and hang them up in cafés and grocery stores. Ask your friends and family if anyone is able to take in your cat. Ask your veterinarian if they have any advice or resources, too.

- Despite what you may hear, listing your pet free to a good home does not mean he will end up in the hands of animal abusers or dogfighters. Free isn't bad. Not screening adopters is. Don't be afraid to ask questions of potential adopters. Why do they want a cat? What are their home and lifestyle like? How will they address any possible behavior or medical concerns? Can they provide personal and vet references? If you're not 100 percent comfortable that this person will be a better home for your cat than you can currently provide, move on to the next person.

- Along with rehoming, you should also try reaching out to rescue groups in your area to see if any are able to help. Even if the rescue isn't able to take your cat in, you can see if they'd be willing to list the cat for adoption as a courtesy while he remains in your home. You can find a list of local rescues and shelters on AdoptaPet.com.

Unless the shelter you adopted your cat from requires that you return the cat to them, **surrendering a pet to a shelter should always be a last resort.** Shelters are inherently stressful for cats. Stress can lead the cat to develop medical or behavioral issues that weren't present in your home. As discussed before, even no-kill shelters sometimes have to make tough decisions when it comes to euthanasia. Sometimes even the friendliest cat in your home can be an entirely different cat in a shelter because the stress of losing its home and being placed in a cage causes the feline to lash out and become aggressive and a danger to staff and volunteers. This isn't to scare you away. I just want to emphasize that you should try everything else possible before you consider a shelter. Remember that open admission shelters are required to take every pet that comes through their doors, so if you can keep your cat out of there, that's best for everyone!

ADVICE FROM THE EXPERTS

Some owners find their kittens through nontraditional methods (newspaper ads, friends or family, Craigslist). What should they be wary of about this process as opposed to going through a shelter or rescue?

When adopting (privately or otherwise), always ask about vet records— has the cat been declared healthy? Has the cat been vaccinated? Has the cat been tested for common diseases? Spayed/neutered? If the cat has not been to the vet, consider the expense of getting the cat completely vetted. A 'free cat' rarely costs nothing. Spend time with the cat or kitten. Do you think the cat will be a good fit for you? If the cat is older, why is the person giving up the cat? If it's for behavioral reasons, what have they done to address the issue?"

LIZ OSTEN
Cat Rescue of Marlborough and Hudson (CaRMaH)

Usually animals through friends, family, or online unknowns are not checked for any health problems. Additionally, you should ask why there are kittens in the first place. Is there a momma cat out there that is just going to keep pumping out babies so the problem persists beyond your one adoption? When I get inquiries about taking in kittens, I usually ask if the mom is alive and with the person. Beyond those issues, just getting the kitten to a vet ASAP is most important to make sure he or she is healthy."

MELISSA SHELTON
Forget-Me-Not Barn Cats

Adopting kittens through nontraditional methods is not inherently bad. What is generally missing, however, is a clear understanding of the kitten's health. If one does choose to adopt a kitten from a non-shelter or rescue organization, it should be evaluated by a licensed veterinarian at the soonest possible convenience."

LARRY KACMARCIK
Blue Moon Cat Sanctuary

> *Be sure that you ask for medical records from vets and ask for any other detailed records of any medical care they received prior to you acquiring the cat. Also be aware that you may not be getting the full truth about its personality, past experiences, or general history, so be patient throughout the adjustment."*

EMILY REICH
Cat Around Town Project

> *I am always wary of kittens bought online or given away for free. They aren't spayed/neutered, dewormed, or vaccinated. This can introduce dangerous pathogens into your home, which could endanger your other animals' lives and health. You also run the risk of your female cat becoming pregnant or of a male cat impregnating another cat. I recommend all people who get a cat through nontraditional methods properly vet the cat and get it fixed as soon as they can. When you go through a rescue or shelter, the animal you are getting will be seen and cleared by a vet, altered, dewormed, and given age-appropriate vaccinations."*

KATIE RIDLINGTON
AK Cat and Dog Rescue

> *Getting a kitten from sources outside a shelter or rescue is helping prevent one more animal from entering the displaced /homeless stream. Things to look for are signs of sickness, watery or goopy eyes, coughing, lots of sneezing. What is the age of the kitten? Is it old enough to be away from mom, which should typically be eight to 10 weeks? Most people don't give kittens shots, so they run the risk of catching a disease before they are vaccinated. Many are not wormed either. A trip to the vet is critical when getting a new animal outside a rescue. Even coming from a shelter, the kitten should be taken to a vet."*

LYNDA STREEPER
Humane Society of Northern Virginia

> *Craigslist or nontraditional ads are fraught with unknowns. These are cats that are possibly sick or worm and flea ridden, and the people who have them have not given them good care. That said, these are cats that deserve good medical care and a home. But their health would be questionable."*

OLIVIA NAGEL
Crystal Creek Rescue

47

" *Adopting from a trusted friend or family member might work out just fine because the adopter can rely on the cat's health history information. However, adopters should avoid buying from breeders, or looking for kittens in newspapers or online ads because the advertiser could be (and often is) unscrupulous, seeking only a cash benefit with no concern for the cat's health and well-being. Also, such sources rarely provide spaying or neutering, vaccines, treatment for parasites, or other essential care. The cost of all of these needs is usually borne by the adopter. A dangerous and heartbreaking result of using an unfamiliar or unscrupulous source for kittens is often a sick or disabled kitten who doesn't make it to adulthood.*"

ROSEMARY TOROK
Community Cat Companions

" *There isn't anything wrong with adopting a kitten this way. Just ensure that they fully vet the animal. Be aware that free kittens are typically unvetted kittens. Vetting can be quite pricy. A lot of the free kittens also come with parasites, which can be deadly for young animals and need to be dealt with promptly. As long as the owner is on top of vet care, those kittens need homes too!*"

KELLI GRAZIANO
The Kitten Nursery

CHAPTER 4

Becoming a Cat Foster Parent

What if you really like cats, but you know you have to move next year? What if you're just financially not in a great place and are worried about affording vet bills? Maybe you think your current cat would like to have a friend, but you're not entirely sure. Or you just want to help homeless cats in need and have a spare room! All of these reasons are great reasons to try fostering. Becoming a cat foster parent means temporarily caring for a cat or kittens while they await their forever home. You could foster the cat for days, weeks, or months. It really depends! Fostering saves two lives: the cat you spared from a shelter cage and the cat who now occupies the shelter cage you freed up by fostering.

Photo Courtesy of Lisa Flanery

Why Are Foster Parents Needed?

By now, you've learned that the shelter is no place to be if you're a cat. After only 30 days in a shelter, cats can start to develop permanent, lasting psychological effects from being kept in a stressful, unnatural environment. But if no adopters are coming forward, what's the solution? It's inhumane to keep animals in cages for prolonged periods of time. What if the cat gets sick or comes into the shelter with an injury and needs time to heal? What do shelters do about cats surrendered for behavioral issues like not using the litter box? Of course, no one wants to adopt them!

The solution is simple: foster homes. If you ask any shelter employee or rescue volunteer what their organization needs the most, they won't say money. They'll say, foster parents. People willing to open up their homes to a cat in need, either short-term or long-term, are in surprisingly short supply.

How Do I Become a Foster Parent?

Cats of all types need foster homes. You could foster anything from a newborn kitten who needs bottle feeding, to cats with medical or behavioral needs, to senior cats, to shy and fearful cats. The choice is yours. Most shelters and all rescue groups are in need of foster parents. I recommend doing a little research on a shelter or rescue group close to you. Read Google and Facebook reviews, go check them out if they have a physical location, and ask around if anyone you know has worked with them before. If they sound good to you, contact them. Some organizations will have foster parent applications right on their website. Others will want you to call or email and have a conversation. Every single rescue and shelter

FUN FACT

Fostering Pregnant Cats

Many animal shelters rely on foster homes to care for pregnant and nursing cats and their litters. Kittens must remain with their mother for 12 to 14 weeks. Foster families ensure that these kittens have an environment safe from parasites and disease and provide human interaction from an early age. If you are fostering a pregnant cat, you'll want to prepare a birthing area for her and block off any hard-to-reach areas of your home, such as behind appliances and vents, so that the cat won't decide to have her litter in an inaccessible (to you) space. Also, be sure to provide plenty of blankets and a private room for mama cats.

Photo Courtesy of Heather Greenberg

needs foster parents. They can never have enough.

It's important to note that every reputable group will pay for all medical expenses. You shouldn't have to pay a penny in vet bills. It varies across organizations, but most groups will also provide you all supplies necessary to foster your cat too. Others require you to provide your own food, litter box, etc., but most will help you out if you just ask. You should also be able to choose what types of cats you're able to help. If you can only do short-term, tell them. If your schedule doesn't allow you to feed bottle babies every two hours, let them know. They should be able to match you up with a cat that meets your requirements.

After you've found your organization and picked out your new foster cat, you'll have to set up a foster space. It's highly recommended that you keep your foster kitty away from any other pets for at least two weeks to prevent the spread of diseases and allow the cat to acclimate to your home. Most people use a spare room, but you can even use a bathroom! I always say, "If you have a bathroom in your house, you can foster a cat." Even if you feel bad about locking a cat away in your bathroom for a few weeks, it's better than a cage, and it is receiving individual care and attention multiple times a day.

A good foster space will have everything the cat needs: food, water, litter box, toys, a bed, and the most important thing: a place to hide. Hiding spots are often overlooked by new fosters but are absolutely essential. This is why you often hear of cats hiding behind the toilet, under the bed, or even crawling inside walls and ceilings when they're first brought home. This can all be prevented by giving them an appropriate place to hide. This could be a covered bed, a carrier, or even a plain old box. In fact, a 2014 study found that cats given a cardboard box to hide in were able to recover faster when placed in a new environment compared to cats without a hiding box. All in all, you should be providing your cat with a comfortable space where he has time to acclimate before introducing him to the rest of your home and potentially other animals. Slow introductions will be covered more in-depth in the next chapter.

FUN FACT
Importance of Spaying

With an estimated 58 million stray cats in the United States as of 2018, it's more important than ever to spay and neuter cats. Female cats can have around three litters of kittens a year, producing an average of 12 kittens annually. By nine months old, most female cats reach puberty and are capable of having kittens.

Questions to Ask the Rescue or Shelter

You've decided you want to open up your home to a foster cat. You have your foster room all set up, and you know you want to try out a litter of kittens. But you probably still have a bunch of questions. A reputable rescue or shelter will be able to answer them all!

- **What expenses am I responsible for?** Some groups will pay for everything from litter to food to medical care. Some don't. At a minimum, you should not be expected to be responsible for any medical expenses. If a rescue asks you to provide routine vet care for your foster, like flea treatments or vaccines, find another!

- **What is your adoption process like?** You're going to get attached to your foster cat. That's a given! So, you want to make sure that the rescue has a good adoption process so that you know your kitty will be going to a good home. Check out their adoption application and see what's involved. Do they check personal and vet references? What reasons would they deny an applicant? Do the adopters come to see the cat in your home prior to adopting? Being familiar and comfortable with their process is essential.

- **What is included in my cat's adoption fee?** Every reputable rescue will require that the cat is spayed or neutered, up to date on vaccines, tested for FIV and FELV, and microchipped at a minimum on the day of adoption. Adopting out cats without being spayed or neutered is a big red flag.

- **What happens if I can no longer care for the cat?** Do they have backup fosters? Boarding options in case of an emergency? I once heard of a rescue that required foster parents to pay for boarding out of their own pocket if there was an emergency and they could no longer keep the foster pet. That's definitely not the norm and is a big no from me!

- **What do I do in a medical emergency?** Things happen, and I've spent many hours in emergency vets with my foster cats for issues from seizures to respiratory distress to severe injuries. How do you get in touch with the rescue in case the cat needs emergency vet care? What is the process?

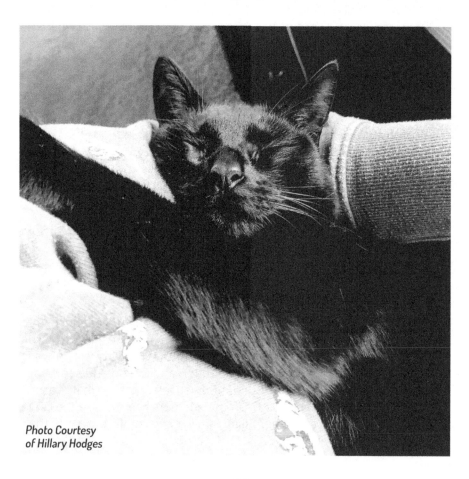

Photo Courtesy
of Hillary Hodges

Photo Courtesy of Patti Drozak

- **Is anything else expected of me?** Do they require you to do your own advertising? Do you have to screen your own applications, or does another volunteer do that? Do you need to take the cats to any adoption events? Are you expected to take the cat to its vet appointments? It's always a good idea to know what your time commitment will be like in advance outside of just housing the kitty in your home.

- **What happens if I want to keep my foster cat?** That's called "foster failing," and it's normal and expected. The goal is always adoption, but there are some cats you just can't say goodbye to, no matter how experienced you are at fostering. Some rescues will have rules against foster failing, usually, if it's your first ever foster cat, to discourage people from

Photo Courtesy
of Jennifer Ryan

using fostering as a "trial run" before adoption. Make sure you check to see what the rescue's policy is before you fall in love.

A good rescue will be friendly and supportive of foster parents. They'll be easy to get in touch with and happy to answer questions and troubleshoot issues. It's okay to try out fostering for a few different places before you settle on the group that you're the proudest to be a part of. In the end, fostering is one of the most rewarding things you can ever do, but it should be fun and easy, and you should feel like part of a bigger team working toward the same goal of rescuing cats. If you don't, move on!

Isn't It Difficult to Give Them Up?

The number one reason I hear that people can't foster is that they'd never be able to give them up when it's time. How can you hand that over that little kitten you've raised from birth? Or that older cat with medical issues that you nursed back to health? If you think you will get too attached, the short answer is that you definitely will. You develop a special bond with each and every cat. While I do understand that feeling and that answer, you shouldn't let that stop you.

When you take home your foster, get yourself in the mindset that this is only a temporary stop on a wonderful adventure. You are the reason that this cat will never again wonder where its next meal is coming from or suffer from neglect. Maybe you were able to troubleshoot some litter box issues that caused the cat to be given up before, and now you can point the new owner in the right direction. You made magic happen and changed that cat's life forever and got it to the point where it's ready for the next chapter.

I can tell you from experience: the first time will be tough. But when you hand off your foster cat to a loving new family, it will all be worth it. When you get that first update a week later with photos of the cat in a big fluffy bed surrounded by toys, you'll feel a sense of accomplishment and pride that is similar to a proud parent sending off a kindergartener to school for the first time. It's okay to be sad or nervous. At this point, I've fostered over 150 cats and kittens. There have definitely been some that I cried over, but the majority I've been happy to send off with families who love them just the same as I did.

If you are really nervous about not being able to give a foster kitty up, as mentioned earlier, there is always "foster failing." But you can't keep them all! Give it a shot because the worst thing that could happen would be keeping the cat. You don't need a lot of space to foster. You don't need a lot of time. All you need is a bathroom to make a huge difference in a cat's life.

Photo Courtesy of Cassie O'Dell

ADVICE FROM THE EXPERTS

Is fostering a cat a good option for a new owner?

Yes, fostering is a great way to find a new family member. The downside to fostering is if the rescue or shelter expects the cat to be returned to them and you or the children have become attached, this can be heartbreaking when it comes time to let the cat go to the new family. Overall, fostering is a great option for all involved, so long as the terms are clearly understood by all parties. And it's very rewarding to foster a cat who was down on its luck until the forever family arrives to take it home."

CHERYL MCMURRAY
Nile Valley Egyptian Foundation Inc.

If you are solely looking to adopt, it's best to just adopt. There is a lot more involved in fostering, depending on the requirements of the state. For example, in Georgia, fosters must have twice-annual home inspections and do additional paperwork. We also offer foster training, and the foster is involved in many aspects of marketing the pet and working with potential adopters. However, if you aren't sure that you are ready to own a pet, fostering is a great way to see what it's like to have a pet in your home without the commitment, and you will be saving a life in the process!"

KIM KAY
Angels Among Us Pet Rescue

Absolutely! Fostering is always the best of both worlds. It allows potential owners to experience caring for a cat if they haven't previously, and they can bond with the cat and further their connection. If the potential owners realize that it is not a good fit or they are not ready for a cat, that's absolutely okay because no adoption has been finalized!"

ELIZABETH FUDGE
Companion Animal Alliance

In our rescue, fostering is not typically a good option for a new owner. Our cats who are ready for adoption—the 'easy' cats—can be adopted from our store location or from a foster home. That leaves cats who need fostering:

- *young kittens (They are cute but are also way more work than most people realize.)*

- *cats with behavioral concerns—especially cats who are frightened or shy*

- *cats with medical concerns that need care in a home setting.*

None of these situations is ideally suited to new cat owners who aren't sure whether they want to, or can, care for a cat. In these situations, if someone wants some practice, we recommend volunteering. Volunteers get to care directly for cats, and the cats get attention and stimulation. Everybody wins. Alternatively, we recommend that new owners just adopt! We provide support and answer questions both before and after adoption. We've never had a cat returned because someone adopted and then realized they weren't ready."

LIZ OSTEN
Cat Rescue of Marlborough and Hudson (CaRMaH)

This is possibly a win/win for the shelters that need fostering. Often, the people fostering will adopt one or two of their foster cats. We call this 'foster failing,' which is awesome."

CINDI CLUM
Cozy Cat Cottage Adoption Center

Yes! Do you test drive a car before you buy it? If you can, I am sure you do. Plus, if the kitty you foster isn't a fit for your family, you still did a great thing! You cared for the kitty until it found the proper fit for it!"

LINDA DIAMOND
SoBe Cats Spay & Neuter, Inc

Yes, it gives them a trial run in their home and family, a good idea for people with children and other pets to make sure everyone gets along and no one is allergic."

DJ SAKATA
Hawaii Cat Foundation

     Personally, I think fostering is a great way to see if living with a cat is for you. It offers the foster parent a short-term commitment but not lifelong as with a full adoption. If this is your first time fostering a cat, an older kitten or adult or bonded adult pair is best. It gives you a wonderful experience with a cat and not the hardships associated with neonates, full families, sick or injured animals. While these are very rewarding experiences, they can be difficult emotionally and physically, and it isn't advised for a first- time cat owner. Fostering also gives you a wide variety of experiences with cats with different types of personalities and activity levels. The hardest part of fostering is saying goodbye, but it is also the most rewarding part."

KATIE JOHNSON
Actually Rescuing Cats

     Fostering is a wonderful experience! If you've never owned a cat before, fostering can be a good way to learn if you can handle the responsibility of owning a kitten or two! You should have a lot of support from the rescue or shelter you are fostering for, so you can ask them questions you have and learn directly from the experts about the best foods, the best toys for enrichment, and the best ways to bond with cats. We have had adopters sign up as fosters after adopting from us, and we have also had fosters adopt one or two of their foster kittens. It is such an enjoyable experience, filled with gratitude for saving lives and the love the kittens give you. Even if you decide to let kittens get adopted by others, you still played a huge role in saving their lives. As a rescue, we cannot operate without fosters!"

AMANDA HODDER
Kitten Rescue Life

     Most rescues are desperate for foster families. Onetime foster-to-rescue situations are a hard sell as on boarding and training are time-consuming and expensive and not a good fit for fosters who are not long-term fosters. However, all reputable rescues will always take back an adopted kitty at any time for any reason! Most rescues have it in their contract that if the adopter cannot keep the kitty, it must be returned to the rescue organization and not given away, put outside, or taken to a shelter."

CORI LYNN STANLEY
Averting CAT-astrophe

" *We do not usually recommend fostering for someone who has never cared for a cat. We provide our fosters with comprehensive training on daily care, behavior, and health, as well as supplies and ongoing support. Even so, a new foster can become frustrated if things don't go perfectly, resulting in upset for the person and upheaval for the cat. An experienced foster is much better equipped to deal with surprises such as a cat in heat, or behavioral issues like scratching furniture or litter box issues. The priority must be stability for cats in foster care, so that they aren't shuffled from one place to another, and only go to a new home when it's their forever home."*

ROSEMARY TOROK
Community Cat Companions

CHAPTER 5

Bringing Kitty Home

At this point, you are well-versed in locating a cat to fit your lifestyle. You know if you'll be visiting a shelter, if it's a good idea to bring that neighborhood cat inside, or if you'll be fostering through a rescue. Now what?

What Supplies Do I Need?

If you've never had a cat before, it can be intimidating to walk down the aisles at the pet store. There is so much to choose from! What kind of litter box do you need? How many? What type of food? Toys? I have compiled a list of the "basics" that you must have prior to bringing your new cat home. Remember to ask the shelter, previous owner, or foster parent what your cat is used to and what it prefers, too, if applicable.

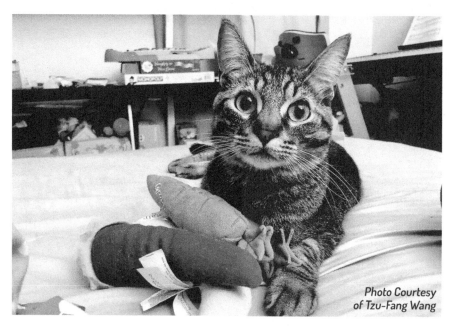

Photo Courtesy of Tzu-Fang Wang

- **A plain, boring litter box:** No, you don't need that fancy Litter Robot. That dome-shaped one with the door flap is a big "no," too. Pick the most basic litter box. A large, flat, uncovered tray works best for most cats. A scoop will be essential too. I personally find metal scoops more durable and easier to clean than plastic.

- **Unscented, clumping litter:** There are many brands and types of litter, but unscented clay litter is the best to start out with. Stay away from crystals, which can be sharp and hurt a cat's sensitive paw pads, and pellets, which are unnatural for cats to use compared to the dirt or sand they would go on if they were left to their own devices.

- **Food and water bowls:** Cats should have access to clean water at all times. A bowl is a great starter, although I also am a big fan of water fountains and puzzle feeders. Choose a metal, glass, or ceramic bowl over plastic, as plastic bowls have been linked to feline acne. A wide dish that doesn't squash the cat's whiskers when he is eating or drinking is also preferable.

- **Cat food:** We'll go overfeeding more in the next chapter, but I recommend sticking with whatever the cat was previously eating, at least at first. Search for a brand with meat as the first ingredient. Stay away from cheap kibble with corn as a primary ingredient, which isn't the healthiest thing to feed your kitty long-term. While you're in the food aisle, don't forget to buy a bag of treats too!

- **Toys:** Whether you have a kitten or a senior, every cat needs a few toys. If you're adopting a kitten, feel free to go crazy in this aisle – you can't go wrong. Regardless of age, you'll need a basic feather wand or fishing pole-type toy and a couple of those little fuzzy mice, at a minimum, to keep your new cat entertained.

- **A scratching post:** Preferably, there should be several of these throughout the house. Cats are likely to use your furniture or carpet if they don't have a better, more appropriate place to scratch. Look for a

FUN FACT
How Many Litter Boxes Do I Need?

A good rule of thumb for litter boxes is to have one box per cat, plus one. Ideally, if you have more than one level of your home, you should keep at least one litter box on each level of your home. Cats can be particular about the placement of their litter box, so try to keep the boxes in low-traffic areas to give your cat some privacy and prevent inappropriate elimination.

sturdy post, tall enough that your cat can extend to his full height when reaching up and stretch out his entire back and legs while scratching.

- **A carrier:** You'll need to purchase a carrier to bring your new cat home in. It's the safest and least stressful way for your cat to travel. There are many types of carriers to choose from, but my personal preference is a large plastic carrier that opens from the top as well as the front. Top-loading, roomy carriers are the easiest to get a reluctant kitty inside!

- **A cat bed:** Comfy places to nap are very important to cats, who sleep roughly 16 hours a day! Your kitty may be happy to share your furniture and bed with you, but he'll also appreciate a place that's all his own.

- **Basic grooming supplies:** I recommend purchasing a good brush, such as a Furminator, and a set of nail clippers if you plan to do basic grooming at home. Most cats do a pretty good job of keeping themselves clean, but regular nail trims will keep sharp claws from getting stuck in your carpet or furniture, and brushing will cut down on shedding!

- **A collar and tags:** Not all cats will wear a collar, but it is a good idea to get one and gradually get him used to wearing it. This is especially important if you plan to let your cat outdoors. However, even if you plan to keep your cat indoors only, remember that accidents do happen. Doors are left open, cats get spooked, and your cat is not immune to getting lost. Tags will allow a finder to easily identify your cat and reunite him with you should he go missing. Even more essential than tags is a microchip, which should be inserted by the shelter or rescue you adopted from. If not, you can ask your vet to put one in for you. A microchip is not a GPS but rather a tiny chip the size of a grain of rice that a vet places under your cat's skin between his shoulder blades. When scanned with a microchip scanner, any vet or shelter is able to read a code comprised of letters and numbers unique to your cat. However, you must register your microchip with your information so that the shelter is able to get in touch with you should your cat turn up there.

- **A veterinarian:** Although this obviously isn't something you purchase from the pet store, having a vet in mind is absolutely necessary. You never know what could happen in the first weeks following adoption, from an accident at home to an upper respiratory infection or kitty cold. It's a great idea to schedule a visit with your vet within two weeks of adoption to establish your new cat as a patient and make it easy to get an appointment in case of an emergency.

ADVICE FROM THE EXPERTS

What supplies or home preparations would you recommend for a first-time cat owner?

Do a thorough check of your home. Make sure there are no cords or wires a cat can chew on, no medications lying around a cat could ingest, no poisonous plants a cat could chew on. Make sure you have a separate space set up with food, water, litter box, toys, and some hiding spots so a new cat can adjust at its own pace (a spare bedroom is ideal). Cats need time to decompress when they arrive in a new home, and they need to set the pace on adjusting. It takes time for many cats, and they need to be given that time and a safe space. Make sure if you have any breakable items, such as figurines or things like that on a mantel, that you understand a cat might jump up and break them. If you are NOT okay with that, put the breakables away."

MARGARET SLABY
Golden Oldies Cat Rescue

This one surprises us still, but some adopters don't think they need pet carriers, or they want to get the cheap cardboard kind from the store. Those are typically for onetime use only, and the older your pet gets, the less reliable those are as the cardboard can collapse, and then your pet is loose in the car, vet clinic, or outside. You want a good, sturdy carrier so you can get your pets safely to and from vet visits, moves, and emergencies. Hard plastic carriers are our preferred carriers."

AMANDA HODDER
Kitten Rescue Life

First-time cat owners should have the basics, like two litter boxes, food and water dishes, a bed or sleeping place, along with various toys. They should also consider a window perch—cats love watching activity outside—a scratching post, several if possible, of various materials. This can save the furniture. Perches on the walls or high up hidey holes, things a cat can hide in but still see what is happening around it."

LYNDA STREEPER
Humane Society of Northern Virginia

> *I recommend buying a cat scratcher. Cats have claws, and they're going to use them. If you teach your cats from the very beginning that there are much more fun things to scratch on than your sofa, you will thank me!"*
>
> **KATIE RIDLINGTON**
> *AK Cat and Dog Rescue*

> *Cat box and litter. If you are a multi-cat household, make sure each cat has its own litter box so that each cat can have the privacy it needs. Toilet problems can often originate when a new cat is seen as a threat to the older cats, who are protective of their own private sanitary facilities."*
>
> **BETTI C. TAYLOR**
> *Magicats, Inc.*

> *Have a separate room or bathroom the cat can decompress in before full integration into your home. People tend to rush into sharing the new family member with everyone and don't take into account that it is a huge experience for the cat or kitten as well. Give it some time to get comfortable before letting the cat loose in your home."*
>
> **MELISSA CHRISTMAN**
> *San Antonio Feral Cat Coalition*

> *Find out what kind of food the cat was eating in the shelter or rescue. Cats' tummies are very sensitive, and they can get sick easily if you switch their food without transitioning. If you would like to switch your new cat's food, you'll want to do a slow transition over at least a week's time. Start by mixing 75% of the original food with 25% of the new food. In a couple of days, you can move to a 50/50 mix. In another few days, you can now have 75% of the new food and 25% of the old. Give it a couple more days before you finally go to 100% of the new food."*
>
> **AMANDA HODDER**
> *Kitten Rescue Life*

> *If the adopter has a lot of breakable items, it might be best to stow them away, at least temporarily. Cats like to get up high, so a cat tree might keep them off bookcases and the like. If the new cat is timid, or being introduced to cats already in the home, calming products like Feliway can really help. Mostly, just give the cat a lot of time to feel secure. It can take weeks."*
>
> **BETSY BALLENGER**
> *Cat Action Team*

" *Cat proofing! Consider things like cords, tall lamps that can fall over (even some bookshelves and other unstable furniture), small holes they can get into (around plumbing or kitchen appliances), and if you open windows, some cats can push out screens. Also, when bringing in a new cat, it's often best to confine it to a small space for the first week or two. This allows the cat to get comfortable in your home and with you before having more space. As far as supplies, you want lots of toys, especially if you are adopting a young cat. Most cat stores have a 99-cent bin, and cats like those toys just as much as the expensive ones!"*

KIM KAY
Angels Among Us Pet Rescue

" *Scratchers! Upright scratching posts and cardboard scratchers. If a cat has things that belong to it to scratch on, it will be more likely to leave your stuff alone."*

AVARIE SHEVIN
Stray Cat Alliance

" *Cats coming into a home need a quiet, safe place to hide. It is good if they can have an area where they can get away from everyone and still be safe and accessible. Many cats enjoy being able to have outdoor experiences, so have an enclosed outdoor area like a 'catio' or try a cat harness and leash to let the cat have some outdoor adventures."*

LEAH CLAYPOOL
Patient Pet Advocates

" *It would be smart to get 'Sticky Paws' and other scratch deterrents before bringing the cat home to start out on the right foot with encouraging the cat to use only the scratching post. The other thing I would encourage is nail clippers! Most people forget that cats need their nails trimmed as well. Routinely clipping your cat's nails will promote healthier nails and lessen the chance of you or your furniture ending up on the wrong side of them!"*

ELIZABETH FUDGE
Companion Animal Alliance

Setting Up a Safe Space

When you get your new cat home, naturally, you're going to be very excited. Who could blame you? You'll be ready to give him lots of love, snuggles, and affection. But put yourself in the cat's shoes for a minute. You were likely in a cage at a shelter, surrounded by scary sounds and smells and being touched by strangers. Then, someone picked you up, put you in a box where you couldn't see what was going on around you, and suddenly you're in a brand-new house with brand-new strangers. You don't know where to go to hide; maybe there are smells of other animals you've never met, and it's scary! Your cat needs some time to decompress.

Photo Courtesy
of Elizabeth Gay

Cats do best if they are placed in one room at first. This could be a bathroom, an office, or a spare bedroom. Just be careful if using a bedroom that you block off places the cat could hide, like under the bed or inside a closet. It is very important that your cat is given a place to hide, but it should be an appropriate place, like a cardboard box, covered bed, or even your cat's carrier. In case of an emergency, it's much easier to get the cat out of a box or shut a carrier door than it is to drag him out from under the bed!

FUN FACT
Sanctuary Room Checklist

When you introduce any new cat to your home, you'll want to set aside a space in the house where your cat can acclimate to its new environment. Here are some critical elements for setting up the perfect safe space.

- Remove poisonous houseplants.
- Provide food, water, bedding, and litter box.
- Lock up medicines, cleaning supplies, and any other toxic substances.
- Temporarily relocate any breakables.
- Use a room that isn't too large—cats love small spaces—such as a spare bathroom.

You want to set up the room with all the essentials listed above. Keeping the cat in this space helps him feel like he's in control and creates a "base camp," or safe spot, to which he can retreat when you eventually give him free roam of your house. Expect to keep your cat in this safe spot for roughly two weeks, then slowly expand his territory from there. Make sure to set up the room prior to getting your cat home. When you get home, place the carrier in a corner of the room and open the door. Do not force the cat to come out! He should be allowed to exit and explore on his own terms.

It's okay to sit in the room quietly with your cat and give him attention if he is interested, but for the first 24 hours, you should leave him to adjust to the new space. If you force any attention or affection on him, the cat could become stressed out and may hiss or swat, even if he is normally friendly. Remember, this is a tough time for him, and you need to take things slowly!

The Two-Week Shutdown

If you've ever adopted a dog from a shelter or rescue, the staff probably mentioned "The Two-Week Shutdown" period. You don't hear about it with cats nearly as often, but it's just as important. Essentially, this is a fancy term for giving your new cat two weeks to adjust to his new environment before pushing any new things on them. Your cat should remain in his "base camp" during this time period. Some cats will want to leave their base camp sooner than two weeks, and some will want to stay longer. Two weeks is a guideline, not a rule, and you should watch your cat's body language and read his signals to know when it's time to move forward.

As mentioned before, this is a scary time for most cats. Your new cat won't know you, and he also won't know where he is. If you were kidnapped and taken to a stranger's home, you'd be terrified. You would not want that person to snuggle you or hold you, and you would probably want to be left alone in your room. Having a proper hiding place in the base camp is very important for a cat during this period. Give your new cat the choice to come out and interact with you, and never force him to come to you against his will. This can damage your relationship and can cause your cat to take longer to adjust and trust you.

Do not allow other pets to interact with your new cat at this point. They have enough to worry about already. Have a conversation with young children before allowing them to meet and interact with the cat, and teach them the proper way to pet him and play with him before you allow them to enter the room.

Provide a quiet, safe place, and give your cat time. Depending on your cat's personality, your interactions with him at this time can vary. Some cats may be interested in playing and petting right away, and others may want to sit in their hiding spot and watch you from a distance. Remember to go at your cat's pace.

This is also a time for you to get to know your cat and monitor his habits. Does he have any quirks? Is he using the litter box regularly? Does he like the food you got for him? Many cats can develop upper respiratory infections, commonly known as "kitty colds," from the stress of moving to a new place, which is another reason to quarantine your new cat at first, especially if you have other pets. It's also common for fearful cats to not eat or use the litter box for a few days upon moving to a new place. Take it slow, and don't rush the process!

ADVICE FROM THE EXPERTS

What's your best advice for the first two weeks at home with your new cat?

Keep the noise level down. Start the cat in one room and visit it often to allow it to acclimate to your sounds and smells. Handle the cat. Expose it to each room slowly in the following days. Don't expose it to the other pets for the first few days, to allow it to feel secure and bond with its people."

DJ SAKATA
Hawaii Cat Foundation

Be patient and follow the cat's cues. The move to your house is a huge disruption in the cat's life, and it can take a while to adapt. The cat might be scared and want to hide. Hang out with the cat. Talk to it quietly. Let the cat come to you."

LIZ OSTEN
Cat Rescue of Marlborough and Hudson (CaRMaH)

If a home is large, with lots of rooms, keep the new cat in one or two rooms to get used to you and the house slowly. It may hide under a bed, so let it hide, and slowly, the cat will come out. They are, after all, curious animals. Constantly pick it up, cuddle it, and always acknowledge it. Show it the litter box and put food in another room. Never let the cat outdoors. If it learns young that there is no outside, it won't spend all day trying to get out."

JUDE EPSTEIN
Much Love Animal Rescue

The first two weeks at home are critical for making a new cat feel comfortable. The owner should be home as much as possible to spend time with the cat and establish a strong relationship. I don't mean an owner should take off work, but he/she should limit dates and appointments outside the home to help the cat learn the new routine."

ANNA SEALS
Central Indiana Foster Cats

▶▶ CONTINUE

Make cats' world tiny and then expand it as they gain confidence. Dropping a little kitten into a big home will freak it out! There is so much to explore and learn. Cats are territorial, so they want to be the masters of their domain in order to feel confident and safe. So, a five-room house will take much longer to feel comfortable in than one tiny bathroom. Start in the bathroom. When the cat seems happy and playful, open the door to allow it into the next room. Don't force the cat; it will come out to explore once it has mastered its current space. Be patient. And play, play, play with it!"

LINDA DIAMOND
SoBe Cats Spay & Neuter, Inc.

Make sure to not leave cats unattended with an opened window! Unscreened windows or balconies should be closed with no access for the cat. But an open screened window for a new cat is also dangerous. Cats can (and do) jump and push the screen out! If a cat gets outside who has only been in the home a couple of weeks before it has the scent of the property and feels at home, it could get miles away and become lost (and starve)—so go out of your way to ensure your new cat does not get out!"

AVARIE SHEVIN
Stray Cat Alliance

Let your cat find one or two spaces where it can go to be invisible, where nobody is allowed to bother it, even if you can see it. Put the litter box in a quiet, low-traffic place, where people and dogs cannot scare the cat from using it."

CHAR RAO
Harbor Cat Rescue

Remember that cats can pick up on your energy; if you are stressed, they will be too. Every cat is an individual, and you have to meet cats where they are. They need time to decompress and figure out how they fit into the new dynamic they find themselves in."

MICAIAH ROY
Community Cat Advocates Inc.

> *Spend a lot of time with your new kitty and be consistent with the rules! I always tell adopters that cats are very much like two-year-olds! They can learn, and they can be trained. Redirection is your best tool! If the kitty goes to scratch furniture, take it immediately to a scratching post somewhere it is acceptable to scratch. It only takes a few redirects for the cat to learn where the acceptable scratching areas are. Wand toys are a great distraction when kitty tries to play with something or go somewhere that is not a good idea. Make sure everyone in the house is applying the same rules, so the kitty is not confused and learns the rules."*
>
> **CORI LYNN STANLEY**
> *Averting CAT-astrophe*

> *The best advice is the simplest advice: be patient. So many adopters reach out after 24–48 hours saying that the cat is not adjusting, and we wish that people would just give them more time to adjust before making a decision to return cats."*
>
> **EMILY REICH**
> *Cat Around Town Project*

> *At least for the first two weeks, any new cat in a new environment will be scared and will most likely hide. Depending on the age of the newly adopted cat, this period may be quicker than two weeks. Older cats may take as much as two to three months to feel comfortable and safe in their new home. Families should entirely expect their new additions to hide. Young kittens are naturally curious creatures. They will adjust easier and more quickly. Give them time to explore. Teach them their limits and boundaries."*
>
> **LARRY KACMARCIK**
> *Blue Moon Cat Sanctuary*

> *The first two weeks of having your cat or kitten at home should be a time of gradual introductions to the household, spending a good amount of quality time playing and cuddling with the kitty to help make it feel safe and secure. Cats and kittens can take weeks, sometimes even months, to fully adjust to a new environment and allow their true personalities to show. At first they may seem very timid or even aggressive with other animals in the house, but they truly just need time, patience, and reassurance to help them settle in."*
>
> **MICHELLE BASS**
> *A Kitten Place, Inc.*

> " *Give the cat time to adjust to its new surroundings and try to be patient. Some kittens will settle in immediately with an almost seamless transition, and other kittens will be shy. They may hide, and they won't show their true personality right away. They are leaving everything that is familiar and safe to them and entering an unfamiliar place with new smells, sounds, and new people/animals to get to know. It's okay if kittens aren't completely settled on the third day, and it doesn't mean they are going to hide forever. Definitely don't be afraid to reach back out to the rescue/shelter if you feel like you and your kitten are having issues with the home introduction process."*

AMANDA HODDER
Kitten Rescue Life

Understanding Cat Body Language

Before I cover the next steps of introducing your cat to the rest of the house, I want to pause and discuss reading cat body language. Cats are normally very clear at communicating. Despite what some people say, they typically do not bite or scratch "out of nowhere." When you bring your new cat home, he'll have a high level of stress. You should be able to understand what he is telling you to know when he's ready to move forward and when he needs more time to adjust.

The four key body parts to watch are the cat's eyes, ears, body, and tail:

- **Eyes:** Pay attention to your cat's pupils. Dilated pupils usually mean that the cat is experiencing a high level of fear, anxiety, or stress. If fully dilated, the cat may be ready to defend himself. Occasionally, the pupils will dilate if the cat is in a playful mood. A direct stare is a sign to back off, whereas a slow blink says, "I love you!" When pupils are very constricted, the cat is likely upset or angry.

- **Ears:** Forward-facing ears indicate that your cat is content and relaxed. When ears are flattened back or to the side, that is a clear indicator that the cat does not want to be interacted with and wants you to move away. Flattened or "airplane ears" are usually accompanied by a hiss.

- **Body:** A tummy display, contrary to popular belief, does not mean that your cat wants a belly rub! Instead, it is a sign of trust and contentment. But be careful – if your cat rolls onto his back quickly with claws exposed, hissing, or growling, it could be a sign of defensive aggression. Similarly, when a cat arches his back, fur flat, likely rubbing against you, he is ask-ing for more attention and petting. But when cats arch their back, hair raised, they are very frightened or upset.

- **Tail:** The tail may be the most obvious sign of how your cat is feeling. When your cat's tail is straight up in the air, he is happy to see you. If the tip of the tail is curled into a question mark, the cat is ready to play. A wagging tail does not mean a cat is happy, however. Cats only swish, twitch, or wag their tails when they are irritated or angry. A puffed-up bottlebrush tail means that your cat has been spooked by something, and a tucked or low-to-the-ground tail means that he is nervous or anxious.

Likewise, you will want to keep an ear out for the variety of different vocalizations cats make. Did you know that feral cats don't meow? Meowing is a learned behavior from being raised by humans and is a sound reserved only to communicate with them. Even cats socialized to people won't meow at other cats. Let's talk more about the sounds that cats make:

- **Meowing:** As already mentioned, meowing is used to communicate with humans. But what does it mean? It can have all kinds of meanings, from "I'm hungry" to "I want attention" to "Hello!" After living with your cat for some time, you'll start to recognize each type of meow and what your cat means by it. Kittens will also mew or meow to their mothers, and some experts have suggested that adult cats raised by humans retain that behavior because they think of us as their parents.

- **Hissing or growling:** Simply put, these sounds mean "Back off! I need my space." The cat could be scared, irritated, or angry. Either way, a cat who is hissing or growling should be left alone.

- **Purring:** Although just about everyone knows that a cat purrs when they are happy or content, sometimes cats will purr to comfort themselves when they are in pain or sick.

- **Chirping, chattering, or trilling:** You will hear this sound when your cat is playing with his toys or when he's spotted a bird outside your window. It's a short sound that sounds a little bit like a cheep or a peep and is provoked by seeing prey. Cats may also chirp at humans when they want attention or when they want to be played with.

- **Yowling:** This sound could be a sign that your cat is in pain or distress, such as when he's been involved in an altercation with another cat. If you have an unaltered female cat, she may be in heat. Finally, you may hear this sound, especially at night, in elderly cats suffering from cognitive dysfunction.

Remember to look at every behavior in context, as sometimes the same behavior can mean different things depending on the situation (such as purring). Although the meanings of vocalizations are important to know, cats primarily communicate through body language. Becoming well-versed in reading body language will make you a better cat parent, as you will be able to understand your pet's wants and needs more clearly.

Introductions to Kids, Dogs, Other Cats, and Other Pets

There may be other family members that your new cat needs to be introduced to, whether two-legged or four-legged. It can be a tricky process to get everyone used to each other, and there are certain guidelines to follow to make sure everyone is set up for success. By now, your kitty has been kept in his base camp for a few days or weeks, and he'll be eager to see what's on the other side of that door you keep disappearing out of. He may be trying to dart out behind you or peeking curiously through the crack.

Put other pets away in another room and give your cat the opportunity to explore the rest of your home. Cats communicate through scent, so allowing your new pet to give everything a good sniff to see what else lives in your house will prepare him for what is coming. You can repeat this for several days until your cat is comfortable with the layout of the home and seems to have sniffed everything. If you have other animals, you can "scent swap" and put the scented items in your cat's base camp to let him smell his new friends as well! You can do this for 30 minutes to an hour a day before eventually allowing everyone to meet. "Forced" scent swapping, where you rub the items directly on the other cat to get their scent, is not recommended as it can cause stress to the cat. Instead, take blankets or beds they've laid on willingly to allow the other cat to investigate.

The most harmful advice you can hear regarding the introduction process is "just let them work it out." Whether you are introducing your new cat to your child, your other cat, or your hamster, just throwing them together and letting them figure it out with no guidance or support is asking for problems. Be sure to carefully follow the slow introduction processes detailed ahead in order to build good relationships from the beginning.

MEETING YOUR CHILDREN

I know, I know. Your kids are dying to interact with their new cat. Maybe you've managed to hold out for this long, but if I'm being realistic, you will

*Photo Courtesy
of Liora Engel-Smith*

probably only manage to hold the kids off for a day or two before you let them go in to meet the kitty. Remember that if you're bringing a loud, unpredictable, fast-moving toddler into a room that you've specifically set up to be your cat's safe haven, you'll need to heavily manage the situation to ensure that you don't set your cat back a step.

Children should never approach the cat first. Have your child come in and sit down and allow the cat to come to them. If children are old enough, they can hold a laser pointer or wand toy, and you can show them how to move it to entice the kitty closer. If the cat will allow it, show kids how to pet the cat gently on his head and back, moving from front to back. If the cat has moved away, he does not want to be petted anymore. This is a great opportunity to teach your child about consent. If the cat says no by walking away, hiding, or hissing, kids should respect that and leave him be. You should always supervise young children around the cat, at least in the beginning.

Having your child be involved in caring for the cat by helping to feed him, play with him, give him treats, and even clean his litter box is a great way to build that bond. Many children will just want to pick up the cat and hold him, but most cats will not enjoy that and will learn to avoid children when they see them coming. Explain to your children that they would not like to be held and squeezed for minutes at a time, and neither does the cat! When looking for a kid-friendly cat, try to pick a cat who seems very confident and tolerant and preferably has experience living with kids in the past. Most cats who are shy or senior cats will probably not be the best fit for families with children.

MEETING YOUR DOG

Dogs, whether large or small, can be very intimidating and scary to cats if they've never met one before. Just as with all other introductions, introducing your cat to your dog should be a slow, gradual process. It's very helpful if your dog has a solid sit-stay cue before attempting an introduction, but it's not necessary.

Some well-meaning pet owners place the cat in a carrier to keep him safe from the dog while the dog investigates. This is sadly misguided. Imagine being a 10-pound cat locked in a small cage with no escape while a 60-pound monster sticks his nose directly in front of you! To make matters worse, you likely already have negative associations with the carrier because it means scary car rides or vet visits.

No, the best way to have your cat meet your dog is for your cat to be totally loose and free of restraint so that he is allowed to make his own choices. Your dog should be on a leash, and if you are particularly concerned about the dog's potential reaction, behind a pet gate or baby gate as well.

Photo Courtesy of Charlyn Johnson

The introduction works best with two people. Have your cat on one side of the baby gate, with one person there to give him praise and feed him treats if he will take them. The other person should hold the dog's leash on the opposite side of the gate, using high-value rewards such as bits of cheese or hot dogs to hold the dog's attention. You will need to read body language at this point. Does the cat run and hide at the sight of the dog? Is the dog intensely fixated on the cat and can't be redirected with the treats? These may be signs that you need to get a trainer involved to ensure that the process goes smoothly and safely.

Photo Courtesy of Bob Bookman

If there are positive or neutral reactions on both sides, eventually, you can allow the dog and cat to get closer and closer over several days, removing the baby gate once you feel safe. I recommend leaving the leash dragging on your dog until you are 100 percent comfortable that the two animals get along well and you don't see signs of stress from either side. Remember not to rush the introduction and that it's much easier to slowly build positive associations than it is to undo negative associations (i.e., if the dog is allowed to chase the cat or if the cat smacks the dog with his claws).

MEETING YOUR OTHER CAT

The best way to have two cats meet for the first time is on either side of a pet gate, where they each have the opportunity to move away if they choose. Your new cat can remain in his "base camp," where he is most comfortable. Remember, just as with dog introductions, you should not hold or restrain the cats in any way, like on a harness and leash or in a carrier, during introductions. Introductions will be very slow in most cases. Expect the process to take weeks, if not months. There are a few basic key steps to follow that work well for most cat introductions:

STEP 1 Scent swapping: At this point, the cats don't need to physically see each other. Every day, allow your resident cat to trade places with your new cat. Put your resident cat in the new kitty's base camp room and allow your new cat to explore the house. I don't recommend any "forced" scent swapping, like rubbing a towel or cloth on one cat and then the other to mix scents. You can bring in a cat's favorite blanket or toy for the other to investigate on their own. This step should take a week or two; wait for your new cat to be totally confident and comfortable exploring the entire house on his own.

STEP 2

Scent swapping through a door: Have the cats on opposite sides of a totally closed, solid door. They will be able to hear and smell the other cat through the door and may even play "footsie" under the bottom of the door. Although some behaviorists recommend feeding meals on opposite sides of the door, I find that many cats find that stressful. Instead, make these sessions awesome for your cat! Shower him with high-value treats like tuna, chicken, or baby food, and playtime with his favorite toys. Keep sessions short, about 5–10 minutes a few times a day.

STEP 3

Allow for visual: Use a screen door or pet gate (two stacked on top for safety) with a blanket over it. The cats should only be able to peek through the cracks. Continue feeding the cats treats and giving them plenty of praise as in step 2. Gradually lift the blanket back, giving the animals more and more visual access as time goes on. If either cat hisses, growls, or stares intensely at the other, give the cats more space and back up a bit until they're able to take treats again. You may need to close the blanket more or go back a step.

STEP 4

Remove the barriers: Once the two cats are comfortable and able to relax on either side of the gate with the blanket totally pulled back, remove the baby gate. Place each cat on opposite sides of the room (10–20 feet apart) and continue to feed treats and have playtime with them separately. Eventually, the cats will meet nose to nose and interact, but they should be fully accustomed to the scent, sounds, and sight of each other at this point, and it should hopefully go uneventfully. If you can't reach this point or you have a setback with any fights breaking out, contact a cat trainer or behavior consultant for help.

MEETING OTHER PETS

Whether you have birds, fish, hamsters, snakes, bunnies, chickens, or horses, consider some of the tips recommended for slow introductions to kids, dogs, and cats. Remember that cats are both predator and prey animals, so they have a strong hunting instinct for birds and small animals and a strong fear instinct of anything larger than they are. Whatever the animal, be cautious and supervise your pets together at first, and ALWAYS keep rodents, birds, fish, and small reptiles out of your cat's reach.

*Photo Courtesy
of Lisa Flanery*

ADVICE FROM THE EXPERTS

What advice do you have for introducing your cat to existing pets or children in the home?

Baby gates are your best friend. I have fostered 120+ animals, many of those being cats and kittens. I always separate my animals with baby gates until they have expressed enough positive interest in each other that I feel comfortable doing a short introduction."

ELIZABETH FUDGE
Companion Animal Alliance.

Children need to be taught how to pet a cat and play with it while being supervised. It's always great to make the children part of the process of taking the cat to the vet, feeding the cat, and litter box cleaning."

CHERYL MCMURRAY
Nile Valley Egyptian Foundation Inc.

With other cats in the home, I always recommend feeding on opposite sides of the doors, then introducing through a cracked door. If screen doors or double baby gates can be placed in a doorframe for introductions, that is a great method as well! We also always recommend using wand toys when introducing cats to get them playing together. Often, if they are focused on play rather than each other, you can get them playing together without them even realizing it initially."

KELLI GRAZIANO
The Kitten Nursery

Cat-friendly dogs are essential to living with a cat. Either they were raised from puppies being around a cat, or they're naturally good with cats (some breeds, especially). However, we've never seen a dog hostile toward cats successfully be taught, punished, or trained out of that behavior once grown."

SANDY, CO-FOUNDER
(CLAWS) Cats Lives Are Worth Saving

““ *It's all about smells and taking it slowly. Best to start with your new kitty in one room, then let your pets smell it from under the door. Then ideally, you can swap rooms so the animals can smell each other even more without the other animal actual being there. If you can put up a gate, screen, or glass door for the first face to face, that is great too!"*

LINDA DIAMOND
SoBe Cats Spay & Neuter, Inc.

““ *For introducing a new cat to children, have children go into the room where the cat is and just sit quietly, or sit and read out loud. Explain to children that they must be quiet and calm and let the kitty come to them. Don't make sudden movements. Don't try to pick the cat up. The cat will tell the kids when it is ready."*

MARGARET SLABY
Golden Oldies Cat Rescue

““ *Some older pets, or pets that have never been around other animals, may have a harder time adjusting to a new addition. One thing that may help is to give your kitten a towel or blanket to lie on, and then after a day or so, you can put the towel in your pets' space so they can adjust to the scent prior to meeting the new cat. Some hissing, airplane ears, and rough play is normal. It could be that the cats are playing, or that your pet is gently establishing dominance with the new addition. You will know when it is not play and when there is a problem. At that point, we suggest resetting the introduction period and extending the time you keep the cats apart to allow your pet more time to adjust."*

AMANDA HODDER
Kitten Rescue Life

““ *Small children should not be left alone with pets. Their interactions should be observed. Teaching your child prior to the cat coming home, possibly with a stuffed animal, how to respect the cat's space and how to use proper touch and play is integral to everyone's happiness and having a well-adjusted cat. When the cat arrives, having quiet time and low-key play with the cat is a good place to start. Teaching children the responsibility of pet ownership by having them help with feeding is a great way for them to build a bond with their new pet."*

KATIE JOHNSON
Actually Rescuing Cats

> *With other animals, scent is key. Isolate the new resident and let the other pets sniff and interact under the door. Brushing everyone with the same brush will help to transfer scent between pets and ease the transition. Introductions should be done slowly and always in a positive manner. Animals feed off human energy, so if you are frightened or nervous, the animals will feel that and may mirror you. Provide favorite food, treats, or toys (playtime) during early interactions so other pets are associated with positive things. For cats, vertical space is safe space. Allow access to high shelves, tall cat trees, etc., so that cats feel they have the ability to get away from unwanted attention from other animals."*

CORI LYNN STANLEY
Averting CAT-astrophe

> *Introducing a new cat or kitten to a home with existing pets needs to be done carefully and very cautiously. Generally, a cat already living comfortably in a home sees any new addition to its territory as a threat. Place any new cat in a separate room with food, water, and a litter box. An older, well-established cat already living in the home will know there is a new 'guest.' Cats' keen sense of smell and hearing is far more intuitive than we realize. Continue the separation for several days. Only under very close observation and controlled conditions should any introduction be done. While speaking in a calm and reassuring voice, a visual and some¬what distant introduction should be made. A little hissing should be expected in most cases. Do not leave the cats unattended until they are both comfort¬able and familiar with each other."*

LARRY KACMARCIK
Blue Moon Cat Sanctuary

> *For introducing to children, it's important to make sure cats don't develop a fear of them. Start the children out sitting on the floor and allow them to pet the cat or hold it. Teach kids how to use wand toys to interact with the kitten. Make sure you teach your children what boundaries look like for animals since they cannot speak. Thing like hissing, airplane ears, puffed-up tails, and swatting, are all signs the pet is giving to back off."*

AMANDA HODDER
Kitten Rescue Life

The new kitty should start out in a separate room from your current cat, or cats, with the door closed. You can start to feed the animals separately on each side of the door. You are looking for them to start playing under the door with each other. They will start to place their paws under the door, and back and forth they will bat at each other. If they're being playful and gentle, they may be ready to see each other for short visits. Keep it short and extend it over time. If the animals seem agitated or frustrated, separate them again. Also, to help your cats get used to the new kitty's scent, you need to give each of them a towel to lie on. Then you can swap them so they can begin to get used to each other's scent. You can also do this by having them swap rooms."

JOANNA LANDRUM
Rutherford County Cat Rescue

CHAPTER 6

Nutrition and Health Care

There is a ton of advice out there when it comes to caring for your cat, and it's really hard to know what to follow, even as a professional working with cats. The following chapter comes with the disclaimer that I am not a veterinarian or cat nutritionist; I am simply sharing what has worked best for me as a longtime cat owner, rescuer, and behavior consultant. Whatever choices you make in regards to your cat's nutrition and health, be sure to do ample research and trust science and your veterinarian first.

*Photo Courtesy
of Michele Fellows*

Feeding Your Cat

Kibble? Canned food? Raw food? How much? How often? What if you have a kitten or senior cat? If you walk into the pet store, you'll see aisles and aisles of food. It's very overwhelming to know what to pick. The most important thing to remember is that cats are strict carnivores. Unlike dogs, who can tolerate and benefit from veggies in their life and even survive on a vegetarian or vegan diet, cats are designed to eat meat and meat only.

FEEDING DRY FOOD OR KIBBLE

If you walk into your grocery store, go to the pet food aisle, and pick up a random bag of dry cat food, you'll likely notice that the first ingredient on the bag is usually not meat. I did just that and found that the first four ingredients were ground yellow corn, corn gluten meal, poultry by-product meal, and soybean meal. Note that poultry by-product is the ground, rendered parts of the carcasses of slaughtered poultry, such as heads, feet, undeveloped eggs, and intestines—no actual meat. This isn't to say that your average bag of cheap grocery store cat chow won't get the job done, but it's the difference between surviving and thriving. If you look at the pet store and choose a random kibble that is a little bit pricier—doesn't have to be the most expensive, but middle-of-the-road—you'll likely see a much different collection of ingredients: deboned chicken, chicken meal, turkey meal, and sweet potatoes were in the bag I picked up.

Dry food is the most common type of food people feed their cats, and for good reason. It's cost-effective and it's easy to feed. In my house, I feed a similar middle-grade food to the example above and always ensure that real meat is the first ingredient listed on the bag. I want my cat's food to be nutritious and healthy, and we all know that corn has no real nutritional value. A medium- to high-quality dry food is a good choice for your cat, but I don't recommend feeding just dry food alone, and here's why.

CANNED FOOD

Cats don't drink a lot of water. Today's domestic house cat evolved from desert-dwelling cats long ago. This means that cats naturally have a low thirst drive and can survive on very little water. In addition, many cats would prefer not to drink out of a stagnant water bowl and naturally gravitate toward running water. This is why your cat only wants to drink out of the bathtub or sink! You can combat this by offering him a water fountain to drink from. Why is it important to ensure cats get enough water, regardless of genetics? Because lack of water intake leads to dehydration, which can lead to urinary tract

FUN FACT
Budgeting for Health Care

Veterinary visits comprise a large percentage of the money you'll spend on your cat. From regular checkups to emergency care to treatment for an ongoing illness, these visits can add up. One popular option in planning for this eventuality is to purchase pet insurance for your cat. A variety of plans are available, some of them focusing on preventative care and others covering emergency expenses. A pet's savings account is another excellent choice for those who prefer not to pay a monthly premium. Instead, set aside a set sum of money each month dedicated to future veterinary expenses, giving you peace of mind and ensuring a healthy future.

diseases like kidney disease, bladder stones, inflammation of the bladder (cystitis), and more. Especially in older male cats, these issues can lead to a urinary blockage, which is a life-threatening emergency.

But back to canned food—canned food naturally contains moisture and is an easy way to add more water to your cat's intake. With most cats being picky drinkers, simply adding a little bit of extra water to your cat's canned food can make a huge difference. This is why I always recommend supplementing your cat's dry food diet with a little bit of canned food or feeding canned food entirely.

Let's do the same test with canned food as we did with the dry food at the pet store. We know that cats are carnivores, and we need meat to be the first ingredient in the food we choose for them. I pulled out a can of one of the cheapest options at the grocery store and studied the ingredients. This time, the first four ingredients were water, liver, chicken, and beef. Even the cheapest option of canned food has better ingredients than the mid-range dry food! Next, I chose a mid-range canned food and read those ingredients: chicken, chicken liver, turkey, chicken broth. Not too different. My conclusion is that it doesn't really matter what brand of canned food you choose; it provides a more natural diet for your cat, with higher-quality ingredients.

RAW FEEDING

Raw feeding isn't something I've personally tried with my cats, but it is growing in popularity with cat owners and is worth mentioning. The appeal is that it's a more natural diet for your cat and more similar to what his wild ancestors consumed. Commercially prepared raw cat food comes in four forms: frozen, freeze-dried, dehydrated, and air-dried. There are many brands on the market, and they may be refrigerated, frozen, or in boxes or bags. Many cat owners prepare the food themselves, but please note that you must do significant research if you'd like to do this, and it's not enough to simply offer your cat raw chicken purchased from the grocery store.

Cats need a balanced diet that completely meets their nutritional needs; for example, all cat food must contain enough of the amino acid taurine. If preparing your cat's raw diet yourself is appealing to you, there are many websites and Facebook groups dedicated to raw feeding. Currently, the U.S. Food and Drug Administration (FDA), Centers for Disease Control and Prevention (CDC), and American Veterinary Medical Association (AVMA) do not recommend feeding your pets a raw diet.

HOW MUCH? HOW OFTEN?

Generally, cat owners will either leave food out all the time (typically dry food) or feed meals at specific times. In my house, I do a combination of both: my cats have dry food left out all the time, and I also feed them canned food twice a day at set times. According to a survey conducted by VetStreet. com, 65 percent of cat owners free-feed their cats, and only 35 percent feed portion-controlled meals.

Free feeding does come with some risks. It's difficult to monitor how much your cats are eating if you have multiple cats. It can also lead to obesity in cats who overeat. However, if we look at outdoor cats who must hunt mice to survive, the average cat must consume at least eight mice a day to live. If we assume that it takes the cat one hour to catch each mouse, that's eight hours a day spent hunting and eating. Naturally, cats are eating all day long, so taking away their choice to free-feed and only offering them two meals a day can be frustrating.

If you worry about your cat overeating, there are many slow feeder and puzzle toy options on the market for cats that can provide enrichment and mental stimulation and slow down eating, as the cats must now work for their food. Putting a portion-controlled amount of food into a

Photo Courtesy of Charlyn Johnson

foraging toy can mean that one meal lasts a cat several hours instead of only a few minutes.

Whatever you decide, be sure to look at your bag, can, or box for feeding recommendations to determine how much your cat should have daily. On average, an adult cat needs 20–33 calories a day per pound it weighs. Use the lower end (20 calories per pound) for overweight, inactive cats and the upper end (33 calories per pound) for high-energy or underweight cats. Foods labeled for kittens or senior cats may be higher in calories than foods intended for all life stages. I recommend feeding kitten food up until one year of age and feeding senior food if possible once your cat reaches between seven and ten years old.

Photo Courtesy of Megan Cullen

ADVICE FROM THE EXPERTS

What's the nutrition advice every new cat owner should know?

Wet food is best. Cats' kidneys need a high amount of water to operate optimally. Natural prey, like mice, is 74% water. Wet food gives cats that much water. Dry food intake means cats need extra water that they aren't getting from the kibble, and cats don't generally drink enough from their water bowl."

ANNA SEALS
Central Indiana Foster Cats

Any canned or wet food is better than any dry/kibble food for cats. Cats are obligate carnivores and must have animal protein. Do not force your ideals on them if you are vegan or vegetarian. Raw has its benefits, but if you make your own food, visit nutritional sites to be sure you are providing all the vitamins and minerals needed."

KATIE JOHNSON
Actually Rescuing Cats

Don't get the worst, cheapest food, but you don't need the really expensive ones either. Don't buy cat food with colors added to it. Cats don't see colors anyway, and it's not healthy. Find what your cat likes. Try a few brands, but best to stick with one kind until the cat gets bored."

DIANE RANDOLPH
Spay Neuter Your Pet (SNYP)

Cats' tummies are a lot more sensitive than dogs,' so whenever you are switching foods or introducing new foods, it should be done gradually over several days to avoid diarrhea. Also, READ LABEL INGREDIENTS! Cats are obligate carnivores (meat eaters), not vegetarians. They won't go into a cornfield and think, 'Yum!' Corn is just a cheap filler. First ingredients should be real meat."

SANDY, CO-FOUNDER
(CLAWS) Cats Lives Are Worth Saving

Watch the weight; it is really unhealthy for a cat to be fat. Provide exercise. Encourage play. Teach cats to walk on a treadmill (they make them for cats). If you find your cat is gaining too much weight, then switch to a lower calorie/lower fat food and increase its activity. You can free feed your cat as long as you are monitoring what he is eating and watch his weight."

LYNDA STREEPER
Humane Society of Northern Virginia

Water, water, water. Cats are not natural-born drinkers and need water to keep those kidneys functioning well. Wet food mixed with a little water is much better than dry food as far as diet."

MARGARET SLABY
Golden Oldies Cat Rescue

Personally, I feed a variety of canned and dry food. A limited amount of canned food, and a bowl of dry food out at all times. And several bowls of water placed in different places. Better to place the water bowls away from the food bowls. In the wild, cats do not eat and drink in the same place."

BETSY BALLENGER
Cat Action Team

Just like humans, good nutrition, especially at an early age, provides a good foundation for a long, healthy life. Always ask your vet for recommendations for the best food for your pet. And always provide age-appropriate food. Kittens cannot grow and thrive on adult food."

CORI LYNN STANLEY
Averting CAT-astrophe

Cats are obligate carnivores. They cannot survive without meat, and they need it in their diet. That is the number one most important thing to know about cats. I personally do not eat meat, but I know I could never put that expectation on my pet. I know a rescue that had a foster that was vegan, without telling the rescue she fed the cat a vegan diet, and unfortunately, the cat ended up passing away. Also, dry food is not great for cats. It can cause a lot of issues like weight problems, and it can cause crystals, which can be deadly, especially for male cats. It is okay if you want to feed some dry food, but please make sure your cat is getting wet food daily."

AMANDA HODDER
Kitten Rescue Life

> *Cats get 90% of their water intake from their diet. This is impossible to do with dry food, and therefore, cats that solely eat a dry diet are in a constant state of dehydration. Even the cheapest-quality wet food is better than the highest-quality dry food when it comes to cats. Feed as much wet food as your budget allows. We see so many cat blockages, urinary tract infections, kidney issues, diabetes, etc., that can be directly linked to feeding a dry food diet."*
>
> **KELLI GRAZIANO**
> *The Kitten Nursery*

> *There are many high-quality foods that provide a well-rounded nutritional diet for your cat. We also utilize supplements such as fish oil, D-Mannose cranberry, lysine powder, and Forti-Flora, depending on the needs of our cats. Fish oil is very beneficial, and we always discuss administering these supplements with our vet prior to using them."*
>
> **SHANNON BASNER**
> *Mojo's Hope/Alaska's KAAATs*

> *Beware of trendy diets or alternative diets. It's best to use an AAFCO-rated brand, which means the food has been through food trials and is nutritionally sound. There are AAFCO-rated brands in all price ranges. Also, many cats are lactose intolerant, so giving them milk isn't a good idea."*
>
> **KIM KAY**
> *Angels Among Us Pet Rescue*

> *When possible, try to feed cats the same food they were eating before they came into your home. If you want to switch a cat's food, do it slowly by mixing the old with the new for a few days. Otherwise, the cat might get a sick tummy!"*
>
> **LESLIE THOMAS**
> *Itty Bitty Kitty Committee*

First Vet Visit and How to Find a Vet

Your new cat is all settled in at home. He's met your other family members, two- and four-legged, and you've decided what and how to feed him. Now it's time to start thinking about that first vet visit. Many shelters and rescues will recommend taking your cat to the vet within two weeks of adoption, even if he's healthy, with good reason. You never want to be the first time your cat sees the vet to be an emergency. Finding a vet in advance and taking your cat for a check-up visit establishes you as a patient and starts your relationship with the veterinarian.

It's even more important if you found the cat as a stray or if the cat was given to you by a private owner. In fact, if that was the case, you should take the cat to see a vet as soon as possible before any introductions to other pets or people take place. As we will learn more about in this chapter, cats can be a host to all sorts of diseases, from feline immunodeficiency virus (FIV) to something as simple as fleas. If the cat has an unknown history, or if the previous owner did not keep him up to date at the vet, a vet visit right away becomes crucial.

If you don't already have a relationship with a vet established for current or previous pets, it can be a daunting task to find one. There are many options out there, and it's not always best practice to just pick the vet closest to you. Here are a few tips for choosing the right vet for your cat:

Look for a Fear Free, cat-only, or cat-friendly practice. These are all designations that indicate that the staff has gone through special training to keep your cat comfortable and happy when at the vet.

- Ask for recommendations! Who does the shelter or rescue recommend? Where do your friends go?

- Check the reviews. Look at Google, Facebook, and Yelp reviews and see what their clients think.

- Call and ask questions. What services do they provide? Do they do emergency visits? On average, how long does it take to get an appointment when you call?

- Ask about fees. How much is their exam fee? Do they take CareCredit or payment plans? You get what you pay for, but it's also important that you can afford basic care or an emergency if one arises.

Photo Courtesy
of Fagan Yusifli

Remember to take any veterinary records given to you by the rescue or previous owner and to bring your cat in a secure carrier for his safety. If you go on your first visit and don't feel entirely happy about how it went, it's okay to shop around! Get a second opinion, or just go visit another practice and get a feel for it instead. Of course, you want only the best treatment for your new kitty.

Preventative Health Care

You know your cat needs to go to the vet...but when? How often? You definitely need to take him once, following adoption, and usually annually after that for wellness visits unless there is a problem. Always talk to your veterinarian about your cat's specific needs, but the following is a generalization of what to expect at those vet visits and what your cat needs throughout the year to stay healthy.

To help with expenses, you may want to invest in pet insurance. Some insurance companies offer a health care policy for your pets that may reimburse you for certain medical expenses and procedures. Pet insurance can cost anywhere from $20 a month and up and generally covers the basics, like preventative care, accidents, and illnesses, depending on your plan. It's important to note that pet insurance won't cover pre-existing conditions, so if you adopt a cat with kidney disease, any treatment for that disease won't be covered. Pet insurance isn't a requirement for cat ownership, but it's worth looking into to see if it fits your lifestyle and budget.

VACCINES

Typically, adult cats need two core vaccines: rabies and FVRCP, which protects your cat against rhinotracheitis, calicivirus, and panleukopenia; both vaccines are given annually. Kittens will need a series of three FVCRP boosters, and adult cats with totally unknown vaccine histories should receive a second booster shot. These vaccines are non-negotiable. There are also a few optional vaccines, such as the feline leukemia virus (FeLV) vaccine, but most of these are not widely recommended by vets.

SPAYING AND NEUTERING

We've already discussed this in detail, but it's important enough to mention again. If you bring home a cat that is not altered, discuss this with your vet at your first visit. Spaying and neutering are considered preventative

Photo Courtesy
of Tzu-Fang Wang

health care, as it works to not only control the overpopulation of cats but prevents diseases such as cancer and pyometra from occurring in your kitty.

FLEA AND TICK MEDICATION

Regardless of if your cat goes outdoors or not, it's always a good idea to have him on flea and tick medication. If you have dogs that go outdoors, they could bring fleas indoors, or if you go out for a hike in the woods, you could bring a tick back in on your clothes. Generally, the best flea and tick medication is one that your vet recommends and prescribes. I do not recommend over-the-counter medications, especially not flea collars.

Despite being marketed for cats, flea collars are generally not safe options for them. Cats can ingest the dangerous chemicals on the collar when they groom themselves, or worse, get their bottom jaw stuck under the collar in an attempt to get it off. This can poison your cat and become life-threatening. Topical flea medication is deposited between the cat's shoulder blades where he can't reach while grooming himself and, therefore, can't ingest the substance. **Never use flea medication intended for dogs on cats, as this can kill your cat.**

BLOODWORK AND FIV/FELV SCREENING

Many vets recommend annual bloodwork be done once a cat hits seven years of age or older to check for underlying diseases, such as heart disease or hyperthyroidism. In addition, blood should be taken at least once in the cat's lifetime to check for feline immunodeficiency virus (FIV) and feline leukemia virus (FeLV).

FIV is transmitted to other cats through deep bite wounds, mating, and occasionally from mother cat to kitten. FIV cannot be transmitted through sharing food bowls or litter boxes or being in close proximity to another cat. For this reason, most cat experts agree that FIV+ and FIV- cats can live together with little to no risk as long as the cats are generally friendly, do not often fight, and are all spayed/neutered. FIV is most common in intact males that live outdoors and are in frequent battles over territory. It affects somewhere between 2 and 5 percent of cats in North America and affects the immune system. Most FIV+ cats are asymptomatic for years and can live long, normal, healthy lives but will be more prone to sickness, infection, and dental disease. Because of their compromised immune systems, FIV+ cats are best kept indoors, fed a good-quality diet, and taken to the vet regularly. There is no cure for FIV, and it cannot be transmitted to dogs or humans.

FeLV, on the other hand, is the second leading cause of death for cats after trauma. Typically, cats will only survive for about three years after a diagnosis. Symptoms of FeLV can include weight loss, poor coat condition, fevers and infections, neurologic disorders, and more. Like FIV, FeLV only affects cats and cannot be transmitted to humans or other animals. It can be spread through close contact with other cats, including saliva, urine, feces, and blood. Grooming and fighting are the leading methods of transmission, but it can also be spread through sharing a litter box or water bowl.

If your cat tests positive for FeLV, it should not be treated as a death sentence. Many old-school vets will still recommend euthanasia, even for seemingly healthy cats that are currently asymptomatic. Ask about the PCR or IFA test, which can be done instead of the standard ELISA test that most vets use in-house. These tests can be more accurate, as the standard "combo" test often produces false positives.

Most shelters and rescues will test your cat for FIV/FeLV before adoption, so you likely won't have to have the cat tested yourself. If you have decided to take in a stray cat, however, have a plan in place for what will happen if you have other cats or cannot afford the extra vet bills that come with these diseases.

URINALYSIS AND FECALS

Cat pee and poop isn't anyone's favorite thing to talk about, but it's generally a pretty good idea to have them tested regularly at your vet. Kidney disease, diabetes, and urinary tract infections can be found by testing the urine, and many common parasites can be found by testing feces.

DENTAL CARE

Yes, your cat needs his teeth looked at annually, just like a human does. Your vet will take a look inside your cat's mouth during the exam and may recommend dental treats or even teeth brushing. All cats will benefit from regular dental cleanings with the vet as well—cats with pearly whites live longer, as infection in the mouth can travel to other parts of the body and cause other issues.

How Do You Know When It's Time for the Vet?

As mentioned before, most cats should go to the vet at least once a year for a checkup and have their vaccines updated, whether or not they're sick. Your vet may recommend a visit every six months if your cat has health issues or is a senior. But how do you know if your cat needs to go sooner?

- **Litter box issues:** Many people are quick to say that their cat is being a "jerk" or that the cat is just mad if it starts having accidents outside of the litter box. But contrary to popular belief, cats don't go outside of the box out of spite. Most commonly, they're trying to tell you that something hurts. When cats experience painful urination or defecation, sometimes they can associate that pain with location, as in being in the litter box. As a result, they leave the litter box to search for a place to go that doesn't hurt.

  Likewise, if you see your cat straining to use the bathroom, having diarrhea for longer than a day or two, or excessively urinating, these are also problems that need immediate vet attention. Straining to urinate can be a sign of a life-threatening urinary blockage, and excessive urination can point to diabetes. Blood in the litter box in any form is also a big red flag. Litter box issues can be behavioral (covered in the next chapter), but if there's a pee or poop problem, the first step should always be a trip to the vet.

- **Upper respiratory infections:** Ah, the dreaded "kitty cold." Upper respiratory infections (URIs) are common in cats transitioning to new homes, especially if they come from a crowded shelter environment. URIs are exacerbated by stressful situations and are recognizable by runny eyes and nose (sometimes accompanied by yellow or green discharge), sneezing, and congestion. Although easily treatable, URIs can cause big problems if not treated in a timely manner.

- **Loss of appetite or vomiting:** If your cat turns up his nose to his favorite treats, that's a sign that something is very wrong. It can be anything from dental issues causing a painful mouth to pancreatitis. Although a hairball every so often is normal, frequent vomiting is not. Your cat could have internal parasites, a food allergy, or even a serious infection. Regurgitation (vomiting up undigested food right after eating) may be resolved by giving your cat a slow feeder bowl, but if your cat starts losing weight or if regurgitation continues to occur

FUN FACT
Identifying FIV

Feline Immunodeficiency Virus (FIV) is among the common health issues for cats. Symptoms of this disease span a wide range of indications and include diarrhea, poor appetite, abnormal discharge from eyes or nose, hair loss, weight loss, and frequent urination. Cats become infected with FIV from other cats. It's essential to make sure that your cat is tested for FIV before being adopted. FIV cats can often live healthy, happy lives with the proper care.

for longer than a few days, it's time to visit the vet.

- **Obvious physical pain or trauma:** Is your cat pawing at his mouth constantly? Limping? Did you see him fall from on top of the refrigerator, or did you accidentally slam his tail in the door? Was he in a fight with another animal or hit by a car? It should go without saying, but pain or injury is absolutely a reason to visit a vet. Also, watch for more subtle signs of pain, like your cat being more hesitant to jump up on the couch, being more agitated than usual, not grooming himself, or avoiding petting and interaction.

- **Skin lesions or missing patches of fur:** This can indicate anything from flea allergy dermatitis (FAD) to ringworm. Ringworm typically appears around the ears, head, and forelimbs and is contagious to humans. It can be a lengthy and difficult process to treat in cats. FAD is generally most noticeable on the cat's back and rear.

- **Bad smell:** If you can smell your cat's breath from across the room, it's time to run, not walk to the vet. Although a little bit of stinky tuna breath is normal, a strong odor is a sign of an infection. Dental disease is common in cats, and an infection in the mouth can actually travel to the rest of their body, causing further issues. There may also be an odor from your cat's skin or ears, also indicating infections. Cats are typically very clean animals, so if they stop grooming themselves or can't keep up with keeping themselves clean, that's also a sign that something could be wrong.

- **Difficulty breathing:** This is a medical emergency. It could mean that your cat has asthma and needs an inhaler, or they could be suffering from something as serious as congestive heart failure. Any problems breathing should be a trigger to go straight to the pet emergency hospital.

- **Unusual lumps and bumps:** When petting your cat, do you notice a lump that wasn't there before? It could be nothing, but it could be something serious, like a tumor. It's best to have the vet take a look and better to be safe than sorry.

- **Fleas or worms:** There are over-the-counter treatments for both, but if you're having trouble keeping them at bay, it's always best to consult the vet and get prescription-strength treatment. Fleas can cause anything from flea allergy dermatitis (itchy, bald patches) to anemia, and worms can cause distended abdomens, diarrhea, and weight loss if not treated.

- **Obesity:** About 30 percent of house cats in the United States are classified as obese. It's a serious disease that can lead to many health problems. It shortens a cat's life span and puts him at higher risk for cancer, diabetes, heart disease, bladder stones, arthritis, hypertension, and more. Talk to your vet about developing a diet and exercise plan for your cat sooner rather than later if he's packing on the extra poundage.

- **Any sudden behavioral change:** Is your cat normally very energetic and outgoing, but now he's hiding in the closet? Does he always sleep in your bed every night, but now he's sleeping downstairs instead? Is he suddenly meowing excessively or biting and scratching you when he never has before? He could be trying to tell you that he's sick or in pain. This is the most important thing to remember—if your cat isn't acting like himself, pay attention.

Grooming and Shedding

Many new pet owners are concerned about shedding and excess hair in their homes. Certain breeds shed less than others, but for the most part, all cats shed at least a little. Even hairless cats develop dirt and oil buildup and will leave brown stains on your furniture if not bathed regularly! Cats like Bengals, Devon Rexes, Siberians, and Siamese tend to shed less than other breeds, but it's important to note that there is no such thing as a truly hypoallergenic cat. If you suffer from allergies to cats, it's very important that you meet and spend time with the breed you are considering first before bringing them home, as cat allergies can be complicated. Are you allergic to dander or saliva? If you're allergic to saliva, you can even be allergic to hairless cats!

To manage shedding, use a grooming glove or brush on your cat at least once a week. If your cat does not enjoy brushing, you can help him get used to it by doing short sessions paired with treats and playtime so that he begins to look forward to brushing. It can't be so bad if he gets treats the whole time, right? Cats generally do not require any bathing, as they keep themselves very clean. If your cat becomes excessively dirty or has developed painful matting in his fur, it may be best to call in a professional groomer. Look for a groomer who comes to you, rather than taking your cat to a shop, if possible. Grooming, when it involves getting out mats or bathing, isn't fun for any cat, and sharing space with dogs and being in an unfamiliar space can exacerbate the stress. It's always easier on your cat to keep him at home for grooming sessions, if possible.

Cats also benefit from regular ear cleaning and nail trimming. You can get a bottle of ear cleaning solution from your vet or over the counter at a pet store. Pour a little of the solution onto a cotton ball, and wipe out the insides of your cat's ears every few weeks. Nail trims should be done every other week or so to keep your cat's nails short, preventing them from getting their claws stuck in carpet and furniture and minimizing any accidental scratches to people.

Nail trimming should be done from kittenhood, if possible, to get your cat used to it early on. Handle your kitten's paws daily and get him used to you gently squeezing his toes to pop out his claws. Reward him with a treat after, and he'll begin to learn that behaving for paw handling results in a tasty reward! If you have adopted an adult cat who is not a fan of nail trimming, try using a distraction. Put down a bowl of wet food or tuna and clip one nail at a time, pausing regularly and giving frequent breaks if the cat becomes stressed or struggles. Cut only the end of the nail, never going beyond the quick, which is the pink part; it can cause bleeding and is painful for the cat. Be sure to use nail trimmers intended specifically for cats, whether you prefer the scissors or guillotine style.

Nail trimming can be a stressful time for cats who are not used to it. It's best to enlist the help of another person to hold the cat still if you can, but you should not force a struggling cat to participate. It's okay if nail trimming takes a while—just do one claw at a time and keep the experience as positive as possible. Frequent breaks are okay! The idea is to build up the cat's tolerance over time, as any force can just make his behavior worse. If you are not comfortable trimming your cat's nails on your own, any groomer or veterinarian should be able to do it for you relatively inexpensively.

ADVICE FROM THE EXPERTS

Do you have any great advice for dealing with grooming and shedding

If you get your cat as a kitten, get it used to being brushed and having its nails trimmed and teeth brushed as a kitten. This will pay off later! It's hard to get an adult used to some of this, but it can be done...slowly. Offer treats when brushing or right after brushing a cat's teeth. I got my cats used to having their teeth brushed by giving them freeze-dried chicken right after (they love it), and now they jump up on the counter and wait for me to brush their teeth so they can get their chicken! If you have a long-haired cat, brushing is essential."

MARGARET SLABY
Golden Oldies Cat Rescue

Cats, by their very nature, self groom and clean themselves adequately. The longer-haired breeds, however, such as Persians and Maine Coons, need regular brushing. Neglecting this ritual will result in matting and twisting of the hair near the body. Besides being a cleanliness issue, this in turn can be quite painful for the cat if not addressed. It is wise to get your cat accustomed to regular brushing when it is young."

LARRY KACMARCIK
Blue Moon Cat Sanctuary

Most cats don't need to be bathed. They are cleaning machines, but brushing and trimming nails is always needed! The best bet is to start the grooming (nails and brushing) when young. Make it part of 'play' and take it slowly. Clip one nail a day if that's all your furry friend can tolerate; don't feel the need to get all the nails in if your kitty isn't in the mood!"

LINDA DIAMOND
SoBe Cats Spay & Neuter, Inc.

It's important to brush or comb your short-haired cat weekly. Medium- and long-haired cats need brushing at least twice a week. Mats, if formed, can pull the skin, and a cat's skin is tissue paper thin, so anything pulling it is painful. I strongly suggest a Furminator for a coat of any length to release any shedding hairs."

OLIVIA NAGEL
Crystal Creek Rescue

Good nutrition goes a long way to help with grooming and shedding! A properly nourished cat should require very little assistance staying clean. Cats are clean animals and hate to be dirty, so they will do most of the work for you. A good regular brushing will provide bonding time for you and your kitty and help reduce shedding by removing loose or dead hair."

CORI LYNN STANLEY
Averting CAT-astrophe

Brush your cat regularly. Daily brushing is essential for long-haired cats, especially in the summer. Carefully trim any mats that may occur. Cats with especially long, thick coats may benefit from a haircut by a professional groomer who has experience with cats."

ROSEMARY TOROK
Community Cat Companions

Pets will never be easy to groom until their owners are consistent, patient, and gentle when it comes to grooming time! Introduce brushing as a positive, fun time filled with treats, and your cat will make it a more pleasant experience for all involved. In addition to this, feeding a good-quality food promotes a healthier coat."

ELIZABETH FUDGE
Companion Animal Alliance

Make sure your cat gets flea preventative every month to prevent flea dermatitis, help keep the coat clean, and prevent tapeworms."

ANNA SEALS
Central Indiana Foster Cats

CHAPTER 7

Troubleshooting Problems

At some point in your relationship with your new cat, it's likely that you'll run into some sort of behavior problem. Whether it's a couple of accidents outside of the litter box or managing your kitten's biting and scratching during play, you'll have to know how best to troubleshoot any issues that arise. It's important to note that any behavioral issue should be discussed with your veterinarian. You may also choose to meet with a cat behavior consultant. You can find reputable cat behavior consultants through The International Association of Animal Behavior Consultants (IAABC) or Pet Professional Guild (PPG) websites.

For severe behavioral issues, such as redirected or fear aggression, you may need to work in tandem with both or consult a veterinary behaviorist. For these severe cases, I strongly recommend discussing behavioral medications with your vet as well. This chapter outlines some of the most common behavior problems you may encounter to help you understand how to combat them.

Positive Reinforcement Works

Positive reinforcement is defined as giving a reward (for a cat, this is usually a treat, a toy, or petting/praise) to increase the likelihood of a behavior recurring. For example, giving your cat a treat for scratching a post rather than your couch will encourage your cat to go back to his scratching post next time. Often, cat owners aren't thinking about positive reinforcement when it comes to cat training. Our minds go straight to "I need to stop my cat from scratching my couch!" when we should be thinking, "I need to show my cat what is appropriate to scratch." Because of this common mindset, many cat owners go straight to punishment-based techniques, like squirting the cat with water, shaking a can of pennies, and verbal reprimands.

Positive punishment is defined as adding something aversive to decrease undesirable behavior. Simply put, it does not work. Squirting your cat with water for scratching the couch does not fix the problem. Cats need to scratch. It's a natural behavior that allows them to stretch out, mark their territory, and sharpen their claws. We are not going to stop them from wanting or needing to perform that behavior, no matter how much they're punished for it. When your cat scratches the couch, you need to redirect him and encourage him to go to the correct place. You also need to make that place more appealing than your couch. There will be more information about destructive scratching later. For now, let's look at exactly why punishment-based training is not helpful or effective in cats:

- It can create more problems. I often hear the argument, "but it doesn't hurt the cat!" No, squirting a cat with water may not physically harm the cat, but it certainly doesn't feel good either. It works to chase the cat away by making him feel afraid, stressed, or anxious. Often, a stressed

Photo Courtesy of Cassie O'Dell

or anxious cat urinates outside of the box, hides constantly, or becomes aggressive. You may inadvertently be replacing one problem behavior with another.

- It can harm your relationship with your cat. Yes, your cat knows that you're the one implementing the punishment, and he can associate you directly with the bad thing. If he runs away when he sees you pick up the squirt bottle, soon he'll be running away if he even sees you. Before long, your cat will lose all trust in you, and you'll have to work to rebuild it.

- It doesn't teach the cat what you want from him. Often, cats don't understand what they're being punished for. In order for punishment to actually work and sink in, very strict guidelines must be followed.

  1. One, the punishment needs to happen no more than two seconds after the unwanted behavior occurs.

  2. Two, it must happen every single time the unwanted behavior occurs (so if kitty scratches the couch when you're not home, you're out of luck).

  3. Three, the punishment must be aversive enough that it deters the cat from doing the behavior, but not so much that it scares him.

Because these steps are nearly impossible to implement in real life, it's likely that your cat will just learn to do the behavior when you're not home.

- It's inhumane. On the grand scale of things, squirting your cat with water is fairly mild. However, I have met cat owners that use physical punishment or scruffing because it's what they've always done. There are products like the Scat Mat that shock your cat when he jumps on your counter. There are better ways to do things. Imagine you have two big tests coming up. If you pass the first one, you'll get a $100 cash prize. If you pass the second one, you won't get anything, but if you fail, you'll be yelled at and have a bucket of water dumped on your head. Both outcomes will motivate you to pass, but I guarantee you'll be more worried and stressed about the second test.

FUN FACT
Training: Just for Dogs?

It's a myth that cats can't be trained. And while the process may look slightly different from training a dog, it can be done with patience and positive reinforcement. The ASPCA recommends two five-minute training sessions per day when teaching your cat a specific behavior or trick. Clicker training is especially effective for cats.

You can teach a cat to do just about anything through positive reinforcement. He can learn to sit on cue, jump through a hoop, stay off your countertops, walk on a leash – the possibilities are endless. If your cat is the "hands-off" type and doesn't enjoy being petted, you can even help him learn to enjoy it by pairing a short petting session with a high-value treat like tuna fish or chicken. You can teach him to accept the presence of another cat in your home by giving him a treat every time he sees the new cat. And you can, of course, teach him to use a scratching post appropriately and stay away from your couch. Positive reinforcement works, and it's a great way to strengthen the bond between you and your cat.

Litter Box Issues

The number one behavioral reason that cats are surrendered to shelters is that they stop using the litter box. Understandably, many cat owners find this to be very difficult to deal with, and some can be quick to blame the cat for being spiteful or angry. But cats just don't act out of anger or spite. Even if we don't understand it, in their mind, they have a good reason for going outside the box. It's our job to figure out why. Is our cat in pain? Does he not like the type of litter? Is another animal in the home bullying him? Once we discover the root of the problem, we can then make a plan for how best to handle it.

MEDICAL ISSUES

Most often, urinating outside of the box is a sign of a medical issue. If your cat is going outside the box, whether it be urine or feces, your first step should always be to call the vet. Most people are aware that urine outside of the box can mean a urinary tract infection, but did you know it could also be a sign of more serious problems, like diabetes, kidney disease, or hyperthyroidism? In older or declawed cats, it could also be a sign that your cat has arthritis or back pain rendering him unable to climb into a box with higher sides. If your cat is frequently squatting to pee, but nothing is coming out, this is likely a urinary blockage, which is a life-threatening emergency.

If the reasoning behind your cat's inappropriate elimination is medical, you might see the following signs:

- Urine spots can be located anywhere horizontal – on the floor, on your clothes, on the carpet, next to the box, far away from the box, etc. Usually, when people report that the cat is "peeing all over the house," it's because the cat is actively searching for a place to eliminate that doesn't hurt. He will often wrongly associate the pain with the location he is in rather than with the act of urinating and, therefore, will begin to avoid the box because he is in pain every time he goes there.

- Although vertical marking on walls and furniture is most often territorial in nature, rarely, some male cats with urinary tract infections will "spray."

- There will be little to no urine in the box; most often, cats will stop using the litter box entirely.

- Inappropriate urination will likely happen every day, nearly every time.

- Especially if stools are very hard or very loose, inappropriate defecation can be medical as well.

- Whether urination or defecation, medical issues happen suddenly, often in cats that have no history of inappropriate elimination. They may be described as "new" or "out of nowhere."

- Accompanying behaviors include repeatedly entering and exiting the box, straining to urinate, crying or vocalizing when in the litter box, and licking genitals excessively. There may also be blood in the urine or stool, and it may smell particularly bad. Any time your cat is in pain or discomfort, he may also hide more frequently or begin to show signs of aggression.

Your vet may recommend a urinalysis and/or urine culture, a fecal, and/or x-rays in order to determine if there is a medical cause for your cat's behavior.

LITTER BOX AVERSION

After medical reasons, aversion or avoidance is the second most common reason cats begin to avoid their litter box. Simply put, this is what happens when your cat just doesn't like his litter box. Many litter boxes sold in pet stores are designed to appeal to humans rather than cats and actually set cats up for failure. Litter box accidents due to aversion are often near the box, on a consistent surface. The urine spots are always horizontal and happen frequently. They can be feces or urine and often occur after a change in location, type of box, or type of litter. Sometimes, a cat will use the same litter box for years and tolerate something he doesn't like, then finally just get tired of it and protest. Let's take a look at some of the questions you may ask yourself if your cat decides he wants to go somewhere other than his litter box:

Is the litter box being cleaned enough?

It may seem obvious, but cats are clean animals. Just like you wouldn't want to use a dirty bathroom, they don't either. I often hear of cat owners that only scoop once or twice a week, and that just isn't acceptable. It's a good idea to clean your litter boxes every single day and a great idea to clean them twice a day, especially if you have multiple cats. Fully dump out and scrub your boxes with mild soap and water every few weeks, and replace your litter boxes entirely once a year.

What's in the litter box?

Cats instinctively know how to use a litter box and do not need to be trained as kittens. This instinct stems from the original desert cats that were domesticated around 7500 BC. Their natural habitat was the desert, so they eliminated in the sand. We've come a long way since then, but traditional clay litter wasn't invented until 1947, with clumping clay litter following in the 1980s. Soft clay litter replicates that original feeling of sand from way back when, and it feels natural for cats to use it. Many cats will not use pellet or crystal litter, as it can be sharp and uncomfortable for their paws.

Generally, cats will prefer plain, unscented litter, as some of the flowery or fruity scents can be too strong for their noses. The best way to keep your litter box smelling fresh is to clean it often! If you are allergic to clay, corn-based litter is the next best choice. Other options are shredded paper litter for arthritic or declawed cats or low-dust clay litter for those with asthma. You may also want to consider Cat Attract litter for cats with a history of litter box avoidance.

What size is the litter box?

When choosing a litter box, look for one that is 1.5x the length of your cat. That's one entire cat length plus another half! Your cat should be able to comfortably turn around in a circle when in the box. If you are unable to find a box that meets these requirements at the pet store, you can make your own homemade litter box out of a plastic storage tote from the hardware store. If your cat is going right outside the box or over the edge, it's likely that your box is just too small.

Where is the litter box?

You should have multiple boxes throughout the home, at least one on each floor, in areas that are private and quiet but not isolated and with clear exit routes. It's common among cat owners to want to hide the smelly, unattractive litter box in a dark corner of the basement, but think about it. If you are all the way upstairs lounging in bed and have to pee, are you going to want to trek all the way down to the basement? After a while, you'd probably get sick of it and move to a home with a bathroom on the top floor. Cats don't have the choice to move somewhere else, so they find a more convenient place to go. Litter boxes should not be in high-traffic areas, but they need to be close to areas where you and your cat tend to spend time so that they are easily accessible.

How many litter boxes does the cat have access to?

Just one litter box is not enough, even if you only have one cat. The rule of thumb is one litter box per cat, plus one extra. That means if you have one cat, you need at least two boxes; two cats, three boxes, and so on. Two boxes right next to each other only count as one box. They need to be spread out in different rooms and on different floors so that they're easily accessible no matter where your cat is in the home. In addition, many cats prefer to urinate in one litter box and defecate in another, so if you only have one litter box in your home, your cat may choose to do pee or poop on the floor instead.

Is the litter box covered?

A study once showed that cat owners with covered litter boxes are less likely to clean them regularly. Out of sight, out of mind. Think of a covered box like a kitty port-a-potty. Nobody likes to use them. They're dirty and stink inside, and they're small and cramped. Covered boxes only have one exit route, so if you have a bully cat, your more timid cat may avoid the box because he feels trapped inside. Similarly, I would avoid self-cleaning or automatic litter boxes, as many of them are inappropriately sized or emit loud, scary noises that may deter your cat from using them. There are exceptions to every rule, but most cats tend to prefer a box that is large, open, and uncovered.

MARKING/SPRAYING

Urine marking in cats is easy to recognize. There's the "back and shake" where he will back up to a wall, couch, or window and urinate standing up on a vertical surface. This behavior is traditionally associated with intact male cats but can occur in female cats and neutered males as well. Spaying or neutering your cat eliminates or significantly reduces marking behavior in 90 percent of males and 95 percent of females. Because this is a territorial behavior, it most frequently occurs after the introduction of a new pet to the home or after a feral or outdoor cat moves into your yard. Typically, your cat will continue to use his litter box for regular urination if his inappropriate elimination is marking.

To combat marking or spraying, the easiest solution is to keep your cat indoors and limit his visual access to the outdoors if you believe he may be triggered by the sight of cats outside of your home. Use humane deterrents in your yard like orange or lemon peels or coffee grounds, or consider motion-activated sprinklers like the CatStop or ScareCrow or ultrasonic animal repellents. Trap, neuter, return (TNR) can also reduce territorial behavior in outdoor cats. If you have recently adopted a new cat and believe

Photo Courtesy of Tara Haley

that to be the trigger, the best course of action is to separate the cats and slowly reintroduce them, as outlined in a previous chapter.

In the interim, always use an enzymatic cleaner like Nature's Miracle or Angry Orange to clean up urine spots. These cleaners not only remove the stain, but they actually break down the urine smell so that the cat will not be tempted to return to that spot due to a lingering odor. Hang tin foil on walls or windows where your cat has previously marked as a deterrent, and consider adding extra litter boxes near where he is marking. Feeding your cat in the area he marks can also discourage inappropriate elimination.

Finally, adding a scratching post in the area may help as well because it gives your cat another outlet to mark his territory. Scratching posts are a visual and chemical way for cats to mark their territory, both with the scratch marks they leave on the post and the scent deposited on the post from the scent glands in his paw pads. As a last resort, you may also speak to your vet about behavioral medication to help your cat feel more comfortable in his territory.

Photo Courtesy
of Nicole Serrano

STRESS

Finally, the last and most complicated reason your cat may go outside of their litter box is stress. Many things can stress your cat out. Here are just a few:

- **New pet or fighting among current pets:** Did you just adopt a new puppy who is terrorizing your senior cat? Have your two cats who've always gotten along started fighting? Watch out for urine outside of the litter box. Cats are very territorial animals, and their litter box is an important resource. If another pet prevents them from entering the room or blocks them from their escape route inside the box, they will avoid the box and seek out a safe place to eliminate.

- **New baby:** A new baby is an obviously stressful event for a cat. An infant causes an upset to routine and also results in new furniture, new sounds, and unfamiliar smells. Plus, the cat may receive less attention from his owner. Often, cats will begin to urinate in the baby's room or on the baby's items in an attempt to get your attention. Your cat is feeling insecure and saying, "Hey! I'm still here, and this is still my house!"

- **Move or change in ownership:** Your cat's territory is everything to him. When he scratches, rubs against furniture, and yes, even urinates, he is claiming what is his. Scent is very important, and cats like for their homes to smell like them. Remember that your cat's world exists within four walls. When he is uprooted to a new home, and nothing smells familiar, it can be extremely overwhelming. To manage stress during a move or when bringing a new cat home, you should limit his access to one room at first and gradually expand his territory.

- **Schedule or routine change:** Did you used to work day shift, and now you work nights? Are the kids home from school for the summer? Did your adult child leave for college? Or maybe your new boyfriend moved in? Cats thrive on routine and predictability, and when you throw that off, you can start to see issues.

- **Lack of resources or overcrowding:** Your cat's resources are his food bowl, water bowl, scratching post, bed, toys, and litter box. If he is sharing these items with other cats, it can create stress. If you have multiple cats, they should have access to multiple, plentiful resources. If one cat's favorite bed is taken by another, he should easily be able to locate a similar, just-as-comfortable resting place. Overcrowding occurs when there are not enough resources for multiple cats, and they feel that they have to compete to gain access to these important items.

FUN FACT
Nail Caps

As an alternative to declawing, which is considered painful and inhumane by most experts, many cat owners are turning to gel claw caps. These tiny, vibrantly colored accessories are slipped over your cat's claws and lightly glued in place. Not only do nail caps prevent your cat from wrecking the sofa, but they also have the bonus of looking cute!

- **Single event learning:** In psychology terms, this means that it only takes one incident to create a lasting association. It could mean that it only takes feeding your cat chicken one time for him to learn that he likes chicken and begs for it in the future. It could also mean that it only takes one instance of him being frightened while in the litter box to cause him to avoid it in the future. For example, if your cat is using his box and fireworks go off right outside the window, he may be afraid to go back to the litter box because he believes it will trigger a loud, scary noise if he does.

- **Boredom:** Yes, boredom is stressful. As I mentioned earlier, life for your cat exists within four walls. If you were never able to leave your house, how would you feel? Cats need outlets for enrichment, exercise, and play every day!

You'll have a good idea if your cat is eliminating outside of the box due to stress if he is urinating on soft surfaces, especially rugs, laundry, and other items that belong to you, like your purse or jacket. Believe it or not, cats urinate on your belongings not because they are upset with you but because they love you. Your cat wants your attention and is communicating that he needs your help in the only way he knows how.

Litter box accidents due to stress can also be accompanied by other behavior changes like aggression or anxiety. Stress can be tricky to resolve, but it becomes easier once you are able to pinpoint what may be causing your cat to be stressed. Play therapy and adding enrichment to your cat's life is a great start and is covered in more detail in the next chapter. Adding pheromones like Feliway or trying over-the-counter or prescription behavioral medication is a good option too.

ADVICE FROM THE EXPERTS

What's your best advice for dealing with litter box issues?

"*Litter box problems can be caused by a variety of things. Some cats don't like specific types of litter. Try different ones. Some don't like the box. Try different styles. Always keep the litter box scooped because a dirty box will cause cats to find other places to potty. We always recommend two boxes per cat and two different areas when possible. Also have a vet check done if cats are going outside the box; it could be a urinary tract infection, stones, kidney disease, etc.*"

LYNDA STREEPER
Humane Society of Northern Virginia

"*The first step is to always rule out medical issues. Urinary tract infections and blockages are extremely painful. If a cat relates a litter box to pain, it is going to avoid that box. So a vet visit is always step one. Ensure you have enough litter boxes for the cats in the home. The general rule is one box per cat plus one extra. Try different litter, different boxes, and different locations if needed. Lastly, anxiety is a common reason that cats have inappropriate urination. Just like humans, cats can have anxiety. Medications that are administered daily can help resolve this for your cat and thus solve litter box issues. Cats can also have anxiety with litter boxes if there is another cat in the home that guards the box, preventing the other cat from using it or causing the cat to fear being trapped in the litter box.*"

KELLI GRAZIANO
The Kitten Nursery

"*If your cat is given a clean bill of health from a veterinarian, it's behavioral, and something is likely causing this change. I will give you some of the causes we found. The litter brand was changed from clay litter to crystals, and the kitten didn't like the crystals. Another kitten was peeing in the sink and on the bed. We ruled out any medical issues and finally figured out it was because the litter box was under a window, and that window looked into the backyard, where the owners had two large dogs. They moved the box, and the accidents stopped immediately. Try to think of any recent changes made, even if they seem insignificant.*"

AMANDA HODDER
Kitten Rescue Life

Destructive Scratching

Now that you're an expert on resolving litter box issues, let's move on to destructive scratching. Scratching is a normal, natural behavior for cats and isn't something that can be trained out or stopped entirely. Scratching serves several important purposes:

- **Nail care:** Contrary to popular belief, scratching doesn't necessarily sharpen your cat's claws. Claws grow in layers, and scratching is helpful in peeling off old claw sheaths and exposing new claws underneath. If you've ever seen a "shell" of your cat's claw stuck in your carpet, you know what I'm talking about.

- **Stretching out:** You're going to want to buy a thick, tall, sturdy post—nothing flimsy or short. Your cat should be able to fully extend into a full-body stretch when scratching. If this type of post isn't offered, he'll likely go to furniture or walls to stretch out his body.

- **Play!** You may notice that during or after an enthusiastic play session, your cat will run to his scratching post to get out some of that excess energy. It can also be a great outlet to expel nervous energy if he's feeling nervous or stressed.

- **Visual and chemical communication:** Scratching is a territorial behavior first and foremost. The actual marks that scratching leaves behind are a visual message to other cats that your cat has been there! Similarly, glands in his paw pads leave his distinct scent behind.

Your cat needs to scratch, plain and simple, but you don't want him tearing up your stuff. If you want your cat to stop scratching your sofa, you have to provide other options that are more appealing to him. We've already discussed how declawing and using punishment-based techniques, like squirt bottles, are not humane or effective options. The best way to find out what's the most appealing surface to your cat is to try lots of options. There are several factors to keep in mind when offering scratching items to your cat.

- **Vertical, horizontal, or sloped?** Keep in mind that your cat is using scratching as an opportunity to do a full-body stretch. He may have a preference for scratching straight up and down, at an angle, or completely horizontal on the floor. A normal scratching post may not be what every cat prefers. Try flat cardboard scratchers or sloped scratchers if your cat doesn't go for a post.

- **What type of surface?** Cardboard, sisal rope, carpet, or wood? There are many different options out there, and your cat probably has a preference for one of them if given the opportunity to choose.

- **Where and how many?** Your cat needs more than one item to scratch on, spread out throughout the high-traffic areas of your home and places he likes to spend most of his time. If your cat favors one corner of your couch, you should have an appropriate scratching item placed near that corner to offer an alternative.

- **Is it sturdy enough?** If it wobbles, forget it. Your cat won't go near that again! Make sure the scratching item can withstand significant pressure, or if it's horizontal, that it doesn't slip and slide.

Even if you've identified your cat's personal preference and what he likes to scratch best, simply offering that to him may not be enough to discourage him from going to your couch. As we discussed, scratching leaves visual and chemical communication signals, and cats are very likely to return to places they've already scratched on to "refresh" their scent. If your cat has formed a habit, you'll have to take extra steps to deter him from your furniture. Remember that when you say "no," to a cat, you have to also find a way to say "yes." When placing deterrents to stop scratching in one place, you should do so in conjunction with positive reinforcement for scratching appropriately in another place.

Many cats find double-sided tape unappealing when they touch it with their paws. If double-sided tape or "Sticky Paws" isn't practical for you, you can also try wrapping furniture in plastic, foil, duct tape, or packing tape. Even if the surface isn't sticky, the crackle that plastic or packing tape makes can deter cats from scratching there. This may not look the greatest in your home, but it's only temporary as you begin to teach and reinforce your cat to scratch in the right places.

After you've made your furniture unappealing, then you can work on making appropriate scratching places as appealing as possible. If you simply deter without reinforcing the appropriate scratching spot, the cat will simply move on to another spot. Making a scratching item attractive can look several different ways:

- **Add catnip.** If your cat is one of the 70 percent or so that has an attraction to catnip, sprinkle it on or near the post to encourage him to check it out. Some scratching items will even come with catnip included for this purpose!

- **Use play.** Play is very motivating to cats. Dangle a wand toy near the post and watch as your cat pounces and grabs on to it!

- **Scratch it up.** Cats are more prone to scratch things that have already been scratched on. Take a metal fork and scuff the post up! You can also gently guide your cat's paws to the post.

- **Buy used.** Just like dogs can't resist peeing on that telephone pole that every other dog in the neighborhood has peed on, your cat won't be able to resist a scratching post with another cat's scent on it. Search yard sales, or ask your friend with cats to store the brand-new post you just bought in their home for a few weeks to get their cats' scent on it first.

- **Reward your cat.** You want to build positive associations with the scratcher. If your cat sniffs it, touches it, or uses it, keep treats on hand so that you can reward the behavior. The more you reward your cat for using the post, the more willing he'll be to keep using it.

- **Ignore unwanted behavior.** If your cat scratches your sofa, your first instinct will likely be to clap your hands, yell, or otherwise interrupt the behavior. As with toddlers, even negative attention can be rewarding to your cat. Keep a bag of treats handy instead and shake it to grab his attention. When he disengages from the couch and approaches you, then give him a treat. That way, you are rewarding him for walking away from the couch and coming to you, not for scratching.

ADVICE FROM THE EXPERTS

What's your best advice for dealing with destructive scratching?

Destructive scratching could be the cat is bored, doesn't have scratching devices it likes, or isn't getting enough stimulation/play. There are a variety of scratching materials. Put out several in different areas to see what is preferred. They also make nail caps to help stop scratching. Never declaw your cat; you leave it defenseless if it ever gets out."

LYNDA STREEPER
Humane Society of Northern Virginia

CONTINUE

> " You can discourage unwanted scratching by affixing double-sided sticky tape to your furniture. At the same time, you need to train your cat to scratch appropriately—make it fun and rewarding. Some ideas: wiggle a 'fishing pole' type toy near the scratching post. When the cat scratches there, praise it and pet it. Give it a treat. You can even demonstrate scratching appropriately when the cat is watching! When the cat starts to scratch the couch, redirect it."

LIZ OSTEN
Cat Rescue of Marlborough and Hudson (CaRMaH)

> " Finding the root of the problem is the first step. Is the cat exhibiting this behavior because something is triggering him/her? Does the cat have appropriate scratchers that he/she can use? What type of material does your cat enjoy scratching? What angle/height does the cat enjoy? Choose the type of scratching post your cat will use. There are a variety of types, sizes, and textures available. Be sure to place the scratcher in a location your cat will use. To encourage your cat to use the scratcher, try putting catnip on the post to attract it. You can also attach one of the cat's favorite toys to the scratcher to encourage the cat to play with it. You can also try the product Feliscratch. This attracts the cat to the appropriate scratching post."

SHANNON BASNER
Mojo's Hope/Alaska's KAAATs

Biting and Aggression

As with any behavior issue, if you're experiencing aggression with your cat, the first step should be asking yourself why the behavior is happening. Cats are not spiteful, and they do not get angry with you, but they do experience fear, anxiety, and stress. As a reminder, do not punish your cat for aggression; he is simply trying to communicate to you that he needs something. For any sudden behavioral change, including aggression, the first step should be a vet visit to rule out pain as the cause. Biting due to pain is especially common in declawed cats. Once pain has been ruled out, we can narrow down what type of aggression you're seeing. Most commonly, you will see one of the six types described below.

PLAY AGGRESSION

According to the ASPCA, play aggression is the most common type of aggressive behavior that cats direct toward their owners. It is characterized by your cat ambushing your ankles as you walk around the corner or biting your hands and feet seemingly out of nowhere and generally resembles hunting or predatory behavior with stalking, pouncing, and chasing. The behavior tends to escalate at dawn and dusk, as cats are crepuscular animals and tend to be most active during those times.

Play aggression is most commonly seen in young cats, but it can occur at any age. Single kittens who are raised in a home without any other cats are especially prone to this, and it can sometimes be called "single kitten syndrome" or "Tarzan syndrome." These cats are often extremely overenthusiastic players to the point of being obnoxious. They do not learn how to interpret body language, how to physically play, and when to stop the game. This type of aggression can be very intense and leave damaging injuries to humans. The following are some solutions for play aggression:

- **Adopt two kittens.** This is the easiest way to prevent play aggression and single kitten syndrome, hands down! Single kittens who are not given the opportunity to learn appropriate social behavior from other kittens turn into adult cats with behavior issues. When two kittens play together, they are able to teach each other bite inhibition, or the art of just how many teeth and claws are appropriate for play. If your kitten does not have that outlet, then you are responsible for teaching him (and you likely have a much lower tolerance for being bitten than a kitten playmate would).

- **Don't use your hands.** Yes, it's super cute to scratch your kitten's belly while he kicks and bites your hands. We've all done it. Now that we've gotten that out of the way, don't do it. When your kitten turns into a 12-pound adult, those bites and kicks aren't cute anymore. If your cat insists that chewing on your hands is super fun, keep a stuffed toy nearby that you can redirect him to instead. You can still play and wrestle together, but the bites go on the toy, not your hand, or the play stops.

- **Biting stops play**. If biting occurs, it's game over. All play stops. And I mean literally – you stop moving. Prey makes noise, and prey moves around and tries to escape. Your hand pulling back looks like a mouse wiggling to get free and encourages continued biting. If you are bitten, be a tree! This means freeze in place. It will be tough the first few times, but it will pay off in the end. A dead mouse isn't as fun to play with as a live mouse, as morbid as that may sound, so make your hand be a dead mouse.

If kitty is insistent, try putting your hands behind your back and standing up. If he is sitting in your lap, do not pick him up and put him down. Just slowly stand and let him slide down to the floor; touching him in any way can be reinforcing and encourage the play aggression. Once he looks away or moves away, then you can bring out an appropriate play outlet like a wand toy or laser pointer. This is teaching him that biting does not make play happen, but calm behavior is rewarded.

- **Encourage appropriate play.** Frustration and boredom are at the root of play aggression. Cats need a variety of enrichment and exercise in their lives. If you can commit to playing with your cat – yes, actively playing with him, not just leaving him some toys on the ground – for just 15 minutes in the morning and evening, you'll certainly see a decrease in unwanted behaviors. Food puzzles and foraging toys are great for in-between playtimes and don't forget about enrichment items like cardboard boxes, tunnels, cat trees, and more. If you rotate toys and enrichment, you'll keep your cat's life busy and interesting.

PETTING AGGRESSION

Sometimes called overstimulation, petting aggression is exactly what it sounds like: your cat bites or scratches you during petting. This is the least understood type of aggression and possibly the most upsetting to cat owners. You, of course, want to bond with your cat and show him affection, and he returns it by swatting your hand away. Experts are not sure exactly the reason for this; some believe it's simply that the petting feels good at first, then suddenly becomes unpleasant, sort of like how you might think it's fun to be tickled at first, but you quickly grow tired of it as the sensation becomes abrasive. By biting or swatting you, the cat is attempting to control when the petting ends. This type of aggression does not necessarily have to happen during petting, but can occur with any type of handling, including brushing, nail trims, or when you pick up your cat.

Although this is the most puzzling type of aggression, it's one of the most easily managed. Cat owners should learn to read their cat's body language and see the subtle signs that a cat is becoming uncomfortable so that they can avoid an attack before it happens. Your cat may begin to twitch his tail, his ears may go back, or he may glance in the direction of your hand. You may feel him tense up or see his pupils dilate. These are all signs that he is not enjoying the interaction. For cats that don't necessarily enjoy petting (and not all will), you can bond with your cat in other ways, such as clicker training or interactive play.

You can work on petting aggression by rewarding your cat with a treat if he allows a few seconds of petting. Touch your cat's head for one second, then give him a treat. Repeat, gradually building up to three seconds, five seconds, and more. Once your cat learns to associate being petted with getting his favorite snack, he may grow to like the interaction more and more. Be sure to pay close attention and read the signals so that you can stop the petting at the very first sign that he is uncomfortable.

NON- RECOGNITION AGGRESSION

The previous two types of aggression are directed at humans. Non-recognition aggression, however, is directed at other cats, specifically cats that the cat already knows and lives with. It very commonly occurs when you take one cat to the vet and leave the other at home. When you get back from the vet and let Fluffy out

Photo Courtesy of Julie Ricketts

of the carrier, then Fuzzy, who stayed home, may hiss, stalk, or even attack Fluffy, even if he's known Fluffy for years. Simply put, it's what happens when one cat appears to not recognize the other.

It's not entirely understood why cats behave this way, but there are many theories. One theory that seems to make sense to me is that the returning cat behaves or smells differently than he has in the past. If he was under anesthesia, he may wobble or walk with a different gait. He may smell like the vet, which the cat who stayed home may find unpleasant or scary. If you have cats who are prone to this type of aggression, ask your vet if you can schedule their appointments on the same day so that they can travel and come back together. You may also want to look for a vet that does house calls.

If your cats are already fighting, you'll want to separate them as soon as possible. Give both cats a chance to cool off and allow for any anesthesia or strange scents to wear off. You can wipe down the cat that went to the vet with cat bathing wipes (I do not recommend full baths for cats) or rub him down with a blanket that smells like him. Treat the cats like they have never met before, and follow my tips for introducing two cats as outlined in Chapter 5. You may be able to perform an accelerated version of this introduction process, but don't be afraid to take it slow.

TERRITORIAL AGGRESSION

Territorial aggression is another cat-to-cat form of aggression. Rarely, it can be directed toward people as well. Commonly, it happens when there is a change in household dynamics: a new cat is added to the group, or one passes away. When it is directed towards humans, it is typically shown when visitors come to the home, whether or not the owner is present. Between cats, signs of territorial aggression can be subtle or obvious. Some of the more subtle signs include body blocking (standing in front of a doorway or staircase so that the other cat cannot go past) or stare-downs. Obvious signs are hissing, growling, chasing, or actual attacks.

Fighting can occur over resources, physical space, or social status. As noted earlier, resources are anything the cat finds important, including his food bowl, his litter box, or his favorite bed, to name a few. If there are too few resources for the number of cats in the home, one cat may feel the need to defend what he feels is his property from the other cats. As a side note, competition over resources can also be the reason behind some stress-induced litter box issues, as one cat may body block a litter box area from another cat. In territorial aggression cases, the aggressor may force the other cat to isolate its living space to one area, which he will rarely, if ever, leave.

If fighting is over social status, fights will probably only be occasional. Research has shown that within one home, cats do not share space equally – that is, certain cats will claim a territory within their territory. Have you ever noticed that one of your cats prefers a certain spot on the couch, and the other cats in the home will not sit there? He very likely has "claimed" that area as his own and would defend it if another cat attempted to encroach on his space.

The most important takeaway when it comes to territorial aggression is to make sure there are enough resources for your cats within your home, distributed in multiple locations. In resolving territorial aggression, adding resources can drastically help, as can separating and re-introducing the cats slowly and gradually. In severe cases, you may need to enlist the help of a cat behavior consultant to help implement counter-conditioning and desensitization when it comes to relationships with other cats or human visitors to the home.

REDIRECTED AGGRESSION

Redirected aggression occurs when a cat reaches a high level of arousal, whether it be from fear or excitement, but cannot get to the cause. Instead, he redirects his aggression on whoever is closest, whether it be a cat, human, or dog. In most cases, you won't be aware of what the trigger was. It could be that your cat is sitting in the window and sees a stray cat outside. As the two cats make eye contact, Fluffy gets more and more frustrated and more and more and aroused. When your other cat, Fuzzy, walks by, Fluffy lashes out at him. This could be an isolated incident, or Fluffy may remember the encounter, and now, whenever Fuzzy walks by, Fluffy attacks him.

You may rush to comfort your cat when he is spooked by some fireworks and runs to hide. However, the cat could wrongly make the association that you are the cause of the fireworks and lunge at you. This is also redirected aggression because the cat's aggression is directed at something that is not the actual cause of his fear and frustration. Redirected aggression can be resolved by separating the animals and reintroducing them, recreating positive associations along the way. If you know what caused the initial reaction, you can make an effort to prevent it from happening again by keeping the blinds drawn and using humane deterrents to keep stray cats away from your yard, for example.

If the aggression was directed toward a human and continues, you might need to enlist the help of a behavior consultant or veterinary behaviorist, as this type of aggression can be severe and difficult to resolve. As with any behavioral concern, immediate intervention is best. The longer you allow your cat to practice the behavior, the harder it is to extinguish.

FEAR AGGRESSION

Fear aggression is sometimes called defensive aggression. It occurs when a cat is afraid and cannot escape. Often, I see cats with fear-based aggression in shelters, where they are placed in a cage in a loud, scary environment. When someone unfamiliar approaches the cage and reaches toward a cat, he responds with aggression because he believes that person may cause him harm, and he has no other option. When "flight" is not available, he must "fight" instead.

In a home setting, you may see your cat display defensive aggression if you use punishment-based techniques like scruffing, squirting with water, or tapping him on the nose. His ears go back, his tail goes tight to his body, and he will hunker down, hissing and staring. Everything seems to lean back, whereas, in a cat displaying offensive aggression, everything moves forward. The cat may begin to associate you with the fearful event and react in a way he sees as appropriate when you approach.

Fear-based aggression, if happening frequently, should be addressed by your vet and a behavior consultant if possible. If your cat is constantly living in fear, that is likely not a great quality of life for him. It is possible to improve and resolve fear in cats through gradual desensitization and by providing the cat with the choice to move away. Desensitization is a very slow process; if rushed, it can actually make things worse, so do not attempt it on your own. Some cases of fear aggression, if they're the result of a cat who was poorly socialized as a kitten, cannot be completely resolved. In extreme cases, discuss your cat's quality of life with a professional and take action to reduce overall stress. This may include environmental changes, behavior modification strategies, and behavioral medication.

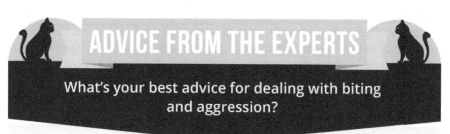

ADVICE FROM THE EXPERTS

What's your best advice for dealing with biting and aggression?

Biting and aggression can be caused by a variety of things. Pain is normally the issue when a cat's behavior changes to biting—either injury, arthritis, disease. Get a vet checkup. The cat could be experiencing mistreatment or bullying from another animals. If you have other pets, watch the interaction, and the same with other people living in the home—some like to tease animals, which can make cats grumpy."

LYNDA STREEPER
Humane Society of Northern Virginia

Biting and aggression can be signs of a bored kitten. Make sure you never use your hands during playtime so that the kitten is not mistaking hands, feet, or people as play things. If you only have one kitten, or the kitten isn't getting enough stimulation from the other pets in your home, it is worth considering adopting another friend. We always say two is less work than one, which may sound false, but it's actually true. Two kittens are less likely to get bored and develop destructive behavior, and they are more likely to have a friend to burn their aggressive and playful energy out with. Kittens also learn something called bite inhibition from each other. That means when they play together and one bites too hard, the other kitten will cry and stop playing. That teaches the aggressor that it is biting too hard, and eventually it will learn to be gentler."

AMANDA HODDER
Kitten Rescue Life

Fear and Anxiety

Beyond the first week or two of bringing him home, it's not normal for your cat to spend all his time hiding under the bed! If your cat is fearful or anxious, he may also have other behavior issues, such as fear aggression or stress-based litter box issues, as discussed above. General fear and anxiety can be genetic, stem from a lack of socialization as a kitten, or be a result of a traumatic event. If your cat spends much of his time hiding or running away, there are several ways to work to improve his quality of life.

The most important thing to remember when working with fearful cats is the power of choice. If you think about it, your cat doesn't have much say in his life. Unless he literally showed up on your porch and invited himself in the front door, he likely didn't choose to live with you. Often, fearful cats are forced into interaction by well-meaning owners who believe that they "just have to get them used to it." This is not the best method.

Imagine if you were kidnapped and brought to an unfamiliar place. Just as you were taking in your surroundings, a giant monster came and started patting you on the head. What would you do? You might scream in terror, run away, hide, or even try to attack the monster. So why would you expect the cat to act any differently? Fearful cats are best left alone unless they decide to interact with you on their own terms.

But how do you get your fearful cat to want to interact with you? If left to his own devices, he may just decide that hiding under the bed is the best-case scenario for the foreseeable future. After all, if a giant monster kidnapped you, why would you ever trust him enough to choose to come out and interact with him? We discussed earlier on in the book how to acclimate your cat to his new home; however, if your cat is especially fearful, follow these steps:

- **Set up a base camp.** Too much space can be very frightening for cats and make them feel like they are out of control of their environment. Starting your cat out in a small room like a bathroom, or even in some cases, a large dog crate can make him feel much more secure. From there, you can slowly expand his territory a little bit at a time instead of forcing him to figure it all out at once. Exposing a cat to a frightening experience all at once is called flooding, and it can be very traumatic. Essentially, it's the same as throwing a person who is afraid of snakes into a pit of snakes and expecting them to get over their fear! We want to use gradual desensitization instead. There is no rush, and the cat can take his time getting used to new things.

  Inside your base camp, you'll want to make sure your cat has all the essentials: food, water, toys, a litter box, and especially an appropriate hiding place. The environment should be quiet and calm, away from kids or other pets. You can use a noise machine and spray Feliway, a calming pheromone spray, to help as well.

- **Appropriate hiding spot.** Yes, your cat needs a place to hide. Studies have shown that simply giving cats access to a cardboard box can reduce overall stress and help them acclimate to their environment more quickly! A box, covered pet bed, or carrier all work well. Under your bed, however, is not considered appropriate. Your cat should feel cozy and secure inside his hiding spot, but you should also be able to easily access your cat in his base camp. If you are using a bedroom, be sure that under the bed is blocked off from access. Also, take care to close any closets and block off any areas where your cat may "hole up," and you may not be able to reach him.

- **Consent to touch.** It's polite to ask your cat if he would like to be touched. Would you just walk up to a stranger and touch her hair? Hopefully not. Hold your hand out a few inches away from the cat. Does he lean forward to sniff? Does he headbutt or rub on your hand? Does he make eye contact with you or move closer? If not, then don't touch him! It all goes back to giving him control of his life and allowing him to make his own choices. Giving choices grows confidence, and being patient will pay off.

- **Use food.** Choose a high-value treat, like chicken, tuna, or baby food. This is a special treat that the cat only gets when you are in the room. Save the kibbles for when you're gone! If he doesn't eat in front of you at first, it's okay. Just leave the treats and exit the room. If he does not appear to be particularly motivated by food, playing with toys may get him to come out of his shell.

- **Interactive play.** Play builds confidence. Engaging your cat in interactive play will help him feel like an invincible hunter, which will, in turn, boost his confidence. Play with your cat every day using a laser pointer or wand toy to encourage him to hunt, stalk, and eventually "kill" his prey. Even if he doesn't chase after the toy and only watches it, you may find that over time he becomes confident enough to come out and interact.

If your cat continues to be fearful and skittish after several weeks post-adoption, you may decide to consult with your vet or a cat behavior consultant for further advice. As stated before, it's just not normal behavior to have a cat who hides all the time. Your vet may want to begin anti-anxiety medication, and a good behavior consultant will know how to implement further behavior modification to help your cat become happier and more confident.

ADVICE FROM THE EXPERTS

What's your best advice for dealing with fear and anxiety?

When a cat is scared or anxious, it's not going to want to do anything involving the thing it's scared of. Let it hide and calm down; it's okay for the cat to not like guests at the house. It's okay that it wants to hide in the closet. Let it. Don't pull the cat out to show it to your friends; it will only teach the cat to be more scared of strangers."

KATIE RIDLINGTON
AK Cat and Dog Rescue

Cats who are fearful may be so for various reasons. Getting a full evaluation preferably by a vet with a behavior background will be a good starting point. An owner may never determine the cause of a cat's fear, however, steps can be implemented to help alleviate their fear, build trust, and help them to live a calmer life. Rebuilding trust with a fearful cat requires time and patience. One of the tools we have had great success with is using Peacock feathers. This is a disposable toy that can be used in various ways. This provides the owner with a way to interact with the cat without invading their space. You can use either side of the feather and engage the cat slowly. This can be used to touch them gently (without putting your hands on them), have them approach you, and refrain from making eye contact but still interact.."

SHANNON BASNER
Mojo's Hope/Alaska's KAAATs

Fear and anxiety can have a multitude of reasons for the behavior. Is the cat older and losing its eyesight or hearing? Has someone been playing too rough or too much? What has changed in the environment? There are many reasons and many treatments, from changing the living situation to medicines that help keep cats calm. Get a vet checkup to rule out any health issues."

LYNDA STREEPER
Humane Society of Northern Virginia

Nuisance Behaviors
(Counter Surfing, Excessive Meowing, and More)

If your cat is keeping you up all night, begging you constantly for attention, getting into things he isn't supposed to, or just being a pain, it's extremely likely that he's just bored. Almost any of these nuisance behaviors such as counter surfing, meowing all night, or knocking things off the table can be resolved simply by adding more environmental and cognitive enrichment for your cat.

WHAT IS ENVIRONMENTAL ENRICHMENT?

Environmental enrichment is altering your cat's environment to make it more compatible with being able to perform his natural behaviors. Essentially, it's "catifying" your home to make it more fun and interesting, in turn helping your cat meet his mental and physical needs.

Cats need designated spaces for resting and sleeping, eating, using the bathroom, playing, hiding, scratching, perching, and more. The more resources they have access to, the happier they will be. Most cat owners get the separate eating, sleeping, and bathroom areas for their cat with no problem, but you should think beyond that. Ensuring that your cat has plenty of climbing, resting, and hiding options in each room of your home will make him feel happier and more fulfilled.

Cat trees, cardboard boxes, and scratching posts are all important, but you can easily rearrange your own furniture to create an interesting path for your cat to travel. Cats like to be able to walk around the perimeter of a room without needing to touch the ground (think "the floor is lava"). Where does all the action happen in your home? Give your cat a high place to perch with a good view of everything, whether it be where he can watch the kids play from a safe height or where he can have a good view out the front window to watch for your car to pull into the driveway.

Scratching areas, controlled outdoor spaces like catios, toys, cat grass, or catnip—the possibilities for environmental enrichment are endless. Your cat's life likely exists only between the four walls of your home. If you were stuck inside your house for your entire life, you might develop behavior issues too. Adding plenty of cool things for your cat to see, climb on, and play with is essential to his well-being.

WHAT IS COGNITIVE ENRICHMENT?

Cognitive or mental enrichment encourages your cat to use his brain. Physical exercise and activity are important, but working your cat's brain is equally or more crucial to keeping him happy and healthy. A bored cat is destructive at worst and annoying at best.

- A great way to keep your cat's mind active is to offer him some of his meals inside food puzzles. There are many food-dispensing toys for cats on the market, and it's very easy to make your own using paper bags, toilet paper rolls, or plastic water bottles. These toys allow your cat to forage for food, which is normal, instinctive behavior. Be sure to start with an easy puzzle and gradually build up the challenge. FoodPuzzlesforCats.com is an excellent resource for this.

- It may go without saying, but social interaction is extremely important for cats! Contrary to popular belief, cats are not solitary animals, and they require and enjoy their time with humans and other animals. If your cat is rubbing on your legs, meowing, or pawing at you, consider his needs. Were you gone at work all day, and this is his first chance to spend time with you today? Were you asleep all night while he was locked out of the room?

- You can appeal to your cat's five senses by offering different types of enrichment. Try playing Cat TV for him so he can watch the birds and hear them chirp (there are many videos on YouTube). Try catnip, silvervine, or other cat-safe plants. Some cats really enjoy the smell of olives and will roll on top of them. Appeal to your cat's sense of taste by offering a variety of different treats and letting him choose his favorite. Finally, touch-based enrichment can come in the form of petting and brushing.

- Clicker training can be a fantastic form of mental enrichment. Teach your cat to sit, stay, even jump through a hoop! Yes, cats can be trained, and most cats really enjoy it, too.

Simply increasing the environmental and cognitive enrichment your cats get will make them happier and more fulfilled, and they will stop feeling the need to perform attention-seeking behaviors. As a reminder, these behaviors should never be punished. Ask yourself why your cat is acting this way and address the problem at the root.

ADVICE FROM THE EXPERTS

What's your best advice for dealing with nuisance behaviors?

" For behaviors we do not like, we have to adapt with our cats or train them! You can teach a cat to not get on the counter by consistently telling it to get off and taking it off the counter. There are also tricks to curbing excessive meowing. I had a foster cat that was all by herself and meowed at my door all night because she was lonely and wanted to be with us. I didn't want to let her into the room because I didn't want her walking on me when I was trying to sleep. She was telling me she was lonely, so I got her a friend. Once she wasn't lonely anymore, she stopped meowing all night long. You have to listen to your cats and figure out what they are trying to tell you!"

KATIE RIDLINGTON
AK Cat and Dog Rescue

" For counter-surfing (also scratching inappropriately), use double-sided tape. Cats HATE sticky. After they have landed on it a few times, you can usually remove it and they remember."

KIM KAY
Angels Among Us Pet Rescue

" Nuisance behaviors can be difficult to address. With excessive meowing, it is important to make sure that the cat is not trying to communicate an illness or something that he needs, like water in an empty bowl. Counter surfing is simply a matter of making the area inhospitable for the cat. Sticky tape, bubble wrap, or tin foil will all signal to the cat that it is not a place it wants to be."

CORI LYNN STANLEY
Averting CAT-astrophe

Carrier Training

Every cat owner has been there. It's time to go to the vet. You pull out the carrier from the closet, the cat takes one look, and he's under the bed. When you finally manage to pull him out from under the bed and stuff him into the carrier, you're already late to the appointment. Although this is a common scenario, it's one that can be avoided with a little extra prep work. Before long, you'll have a cat who goes into his carrier willingly and maybe even on cue! You'll need to follow these tips far in advance of your vet visit, but the extra preparation will go a long way.

1. The best type of carrier by far is a hard plastic carrier with a front door and a top door. You want it to be roomy and comfortable, large enough that your cat can turn in a circle. I don't recommend soft carriers because they can be more difficult to clean and more difficult to get your cat inside. Top doors make it much easier to place your cat in the carrier rather than stuffing him through the front door.

2. Leave your carrier out in plain sight all the time. If your cat is triggered by the sight of the carrier, make it boring. If he passes by it in the living room every single day, it will gradually lose the scariness and the association that if he sees it, it means something unpleasant is going to happen. You can even pick it up and move it around from time to time to further desensitize your cat.

3. Make the carrier appealing. Add cozy blankets or a bed inside and spray them with Feliway. Leave tasty treats or new toys inside for your cat to find. Soon, he will be going up to investigate the carrier to see what fun surprise you've left for him this time! You may even catch him going inside for a nap before long.

4. After your cat is comfortable with the sight of the carrier and will go inside willingly to get a treat, begin closing the door behind him. Leave him closed in for just a few seconds at first, then gradually leave him closed inside for longer and longer. Remember that if he becomes distressed at any time, you're no longer teaching him to love going inside his carrier.

5. At this point, you can start teaching the cat to go inside on cue. Toss a treat to the back of the carrier and say "carrier" or "go in," whatever you prefer. You can also blow a whistle if you'd like. Repeat this every time, and before long, you can blow your whistle from the kitchen, and the cat will come running from the bedroom to go in his carrier and get his treat!

6. Start taking your cat for frequent, short trips inside his carrier. At first, you can just walk him around the house. Then walk him outside to the mailbox and back. Then, take a car ride around the block and back. You want him to learn that carrier rides don't always end in an unpleasant vet visit.

If you need to take your cat to the vet before you have a chance to enact this training pattern, try to place the carrier out in plain sight at least 24 hours in advance of the vet visit. If you anticipate there being an issue, gently wrap your cat in a blanket or towel and lower him, hind legs first, into the carrier (if there is not a top door, place the carrier front door facing up). This is the least stressful method for everyone involved, and the blanket prevents any claws from getting to you on purpose or by accident.

ADVICE FROM THE EXPERTS

What's your best advice for helping with carrier training?

Put treats in an open carrier that the cat will only get if it goes in. Never shut the door. This teaches the cat if it goes in and out, it is not like a prison. Once the cat is comfortable, shut the door a few minutes at a time until it is secure in knowing it will get to come back out. If getting into a carrier is almost impossible, we recommend two things. First, a top-loading and front-loading carrier. Second, if the cat still won't let you put it in head first, back it in. We have never had a problem backing a cat in."

CINDI CLUM
Cozy Cat Cottage Adoption Center

Believe it or not, you can crate train a cat! Some cats think, 'Carriers take me scary places, so I don't like them.' You have to make the carrier a great experience for them! Leave it in your living room for the cats to nap in. Sneak some treats in there so when they go in, they find something tasty! You'll see cats want to go in the carrier, and they won't be scared of it or put up a fight to go into it when they need to."

KATIE RIDLINGTON
AK Cat and Dog Rescue

Photo Courtesy
of Megan Cullen

Giving Medication

Inevitably, there will be a point in your cat's life where he requires medication. It could be a one-time thing or a lifelong process, but one thing is for sure—giving cats pills is no fun. Nobody wants to wrestle with their cat and force medication down his throat, especially not every day for the rest of his life. Here are a few tips I've compiled after medicating quite a few cats in my lifetime.

- **Ask for transdermal or liquid.** Pilling an unwilling cat is tough, no matter who you are. If your vet only carries a pill for your cat, ask about having the medication compounded at a local pharmacy. Many local pharmacies can make any medication into a liquid form, and some can even flavor them with tuna or chicken! Squirt a little bit of that medication disguised as tuna juice onto a morsel of tasty wet food, and it becomes a breeze! If you have a picky eater, ask about transdermal. This type of medication comes in a cream form that is absorbed through the skin. Just dab a little bit on the inside of your cat's ear, and he is good to go.

- **Crush, crush, crush.** If transdermal and liquid are not options, invest in a pill crusher (or empty the capsule). Grind up that pill into dust and try to sprinkle that in some tuna juice or chicken broth. Suck it up in a syringe and give it to your cat that way or try disguising it in food.

- **Make a sandwich.** The more upset and worked up you get about medication time, the worse your cat will respond. So, start positive, and end positive, sandwiching the bad stuff right in the middle. It looks like this: treat, treat, treat, medication, treat, treat, treat. If you outweigh the negative with the positive, your cat won't mind quite as much.

- **Get familiar.** Use your syringe or pill gun to deliver yummy treats to your cat, too. If your cat learns that the syringe predicts chicken baby food nine times out of ten, he will always come running when he sees you get it out. Start by using it to put dabs of the baby food on the floor, then build up to using it to put the treat directly into the cat's mouth. You can do the same with hard treats or bits of chicken in the pill gun.

- **If all else fails,** please don't use the scruff and shove method unless you have no other options. Have a friend wrap kitty up in a towel or blanket, keeping the sharp parts of the cat nestled safely inside. With your friend holding the cat tightly, open his mouth and deposit the medication as far back into the mouth as you can. Finish the session by rewarding your cat profusely with his favorite treats. The more pleasant you can possibly make this unpleasant experience, the more compliant your cat will be in the future!

ADVICE FROM THE EXPERTS

What's your best advice for help with giving medication?

Good luck trying to get a pill down a cat's throat. Try crushing the pill and dissolving it in a very small amount of water. It is then easily sucked up in a syringe and given to the cat that way."

LARRY KACMARCIK
Blue Moon Cat Sanctuary

Try pill pockets. Cats seem to like the dog ones better than the cat ones. You can break off pieces since they are bigger. I usually just use my finger to push it gently to the back of the throat, hold the cat's mouth closed (also gently), and blow in its face (which makes it swallow). You can try to hide medication in food, but most cats are too smart for that and won't eat any of it. Then you've wasted the pill."

KIM KAY
Angels Among Us Pet Rescue

Administering medication can cause owners stress as they anticipate how to give it to their cat. The process of giving medication should be done in a way that is positive based, fear/free, and with minimal stress. In our program, we have multiple cats who receive medication several times a day. One of our cats has a seizure disorder and requires his medication administered three times a day with a syringe. To help him associate the syringe with something positive, we use treats such as Temptations or Churu treats. We first got him used to the syringe by his face and gave him a treat right afterward or played with him with his favorite toy. He has a routine now, where he runs to one of the cat trees, waits for his syringe, and I administer it, then he gets his treat afterward."

SHANNON BASNER
Mojo's Hope/Alaska's KAAATs

CHAPTER 8

Playtime and Enrichment

We are nearing the end of this book, and if you've been following along so far, you should be well aware that cats are not the low-maintenance pets that many people make them out to be. Cats are finally starting to get their time in the spotlight, whereas before, it was strongly believed by the general public that cats were antisocial and lazy. Now, we know better. Your cat requires play and enrichment, whether he's a kitten or super senior. Play is the most natural thing a cat can do in an unnatural environment. Spending just 10–15 minutes twice a day playing with your cat will decrease problem behaviors and fulfill your cat's internal, innate need to hunt and catch prey.

Play Therapy

No, throwing down a couple of toy mice on the floor of your living room is not playing with your cat! Toys on the floor are "dead" and boring to cats, who want to chase live, active prey. Play should be interactive and simulate hunting, simultaneously working their bodies and their brains for double the stimulation. Besides being one of the most fulfilling activities for your cat, it's also a great way to bond with those cats who aren't necessarily fond of being held or petted.

I know what you're going to say next. "I've tried to play with my cat. He doesn't play with toys!" Wrong. If your cat isn't playing with toys, it's either time to take him to the vet for a check-up, or it's human error—you're just not playing with him correctly. Some cats are "specialized" hunters, meaning they prefer a certain type of prey to another. You may or may not have noticed that many cat toys on the market tend to simulate a certain type of prey. Either there are feathers (i.e., a bird) or a stuffed mouse attached at the end of the string. Or maybe there's just a string (simulating a snake). How you move the toy (around in the air, pausing for a few seconds to land like a bird, or slithering it around, peeking it out from behind corners like a snake) can also wake up a preferred prey instinct in your cat as well.

TIPS FOR PLAYING WITH YOUR CAT:

- **Laser pointers** can be great when used correctly. However, they are prone to causing frustration in kitties, who love the thrill of the chase at first, but quickly realize that the laser is prey that can never be caught. It's a game that they can never actually win. But you can combat this frustration by setting up a room full of toys and hidden treats and bringing your cat in to play. By pausing the laser pointer at a toy or spot where a treat is hidden, you're giving your cat an opportunity to pounce on something physical and maybe even get a tasty snack out of it. Of note, laser pointers are not appropriate for homes with dogs, as they have been proven to cause irreversible neurotic and compulsive behaviors.

- **Novelty is important.** Variety is the spice of life! If your cat just has the same old toy to play with all the time, of course, he's not going to be interested in it after a while. You don't need to go crazy at the pet store

*Photo Courtesy
of Jennifer Boaro*

Photo Courtesy of Jennifer Ryan

buying him new toys every week. Consider rotating toys instead, where you keep out a few toys one week, then put them away and bring out a new set of toys the next week. This keeps all of your cat's toys novel and interesting and holds his interest long-term. Of course, if your cat has a favorite toy that he loves, there is no need to take one away from him.

- **Difficulty level** should be considered when playing. Not too easy, not too hard. Your cat should always be allowed to win the game, but it's okay if they have to work for it first. Alternate the speed of movement, drag the toy under or over an obstacle, move it along until it's just out of sight behind a corner, and always keep the toy moving away from your cat. Real prey is never going to walk right up and park itself under your cat's nose! The more techniques you try, the more you'll get to know what your cat prefers. Keep the game a little easier for young kittens, who are still learning, and for senior cats, who may not be able to move like they used to.

- **Appeal to his senses.** Play is primarily visual, but don't be afraid to involve the other four senses as well. Add scents like fresh catnip or silvervine to the toy right before playtime. Choose a toy that chirps, crinkles, or jingles. Incorporate treats into playtime by tossing your cat a couple when he "catches his prey." This will reinforce to him that he is a successful hunter! Finally, try out a variety of toys that feel different to the touch, whether they are made from felt, plastic, cardboard, mylar, or something else.

- **Timing matters.** Cats are crepuscular, so they are most active at dawn and dusk. Your cat will be most motivated to play during those times! Make it work to your advantage, and tire your kitty out right before you head off to work for the day again when you're ready to call it a night.

137

Food Puzzles

If you don't have at least a couple of food puzzles for your cat, when you finish reading this, drop what you're doing and head out to make it happen. First, what is a food puzzle? If you're like most cat owners, you probably pour some kibble into a bowl for your cat and call it a day. This is fine (and normal). But are you really making the most out of your cat's mealtime? If you've paid any attention so far, you've heard me discuss how important it is to keep life inside the four walls interesting and exciting for your cat. Mental and physical enrichment is so important, and food puzzles allow you to provide the best of both worlds for your cat, with very little effort on your part!

A food puzzle can be anything from a toilet paper roll folded in with holes poked in it to a complex store-bought feeder with multiple levers, buttons, and knobs. Simply put, it's a type of toy that allows your cat to forage and work for his food rather than be served it in a bowl. If your cat had to survive on his own outside, he'd spend the majority of his day hunting. Indoors, your cat takes a quick stroll over to the kitchen, and mealtime is over in about five minutes. You can't spend the majority of your day playing with your cat to encourage those natural hunting behaviors and keep him busy and fulfilled, so allow the puzzle feeder to do the work for you. In addition to encouraging natural behavior in your cat, food puzzles can also serve as a tool to help with weight loss, as they encourage physical activity and slow down eating.

Current research says that cats will still choose to eat out of a bowl if given the option between a bowl and a puzzle feeder, so it's important to find the balance between enriching your cat's life and providing him with a source of added frustration. Start slow, and make it easy at first. Don't exclusively feed all of your cat's food using puzzles. About half of your cat's daily intake, plus treats, is appropriate. Remember that naturally, if given a choice, cats will eat multiple small meals per day, and the traditional two

> ## FUN FACT
> ### Catios
>
> Indoor cats live an average of 10 to 15 years, while their outdoor counterparts live an average of two to five. The safest option for allowing your indoor cat to experience the great outdoors is to build a catio. Catios are enclosed outdoor spaces, usually made with a wood or metal frame and enclosed by wire mesh. These safe, outdoor habitats run the gamut from portable pop-ups to multi-level penthouses accessible via a kitty door. Entertainment, fresh air, and mental stimulation are all benefits of the catio. There is a wealth of tutorials to build your very own catio of your dreams.

meals a day setup can be frustrating for some. Food puzzles give you the opportunity to break it up so that your cat can eat multiple times throughout the day, as he is less likely to consume the whole meal at once like he would from a bowl.

EASY HOMEMADE PUZZLES:

- Take an empty toilet paper roll and fold in the corners. Use scissors to poke several holes in the tube. The more holes and the larger they are, the easier the game will be. Fill the tube with dry food. Your cat must either bat the tube around or tear it open to get to the food inside.

- Fill an ice cube tray with dry or wet food.

- Poke holes in a plastic water bottle using scissors and fill the bottle with dry food or treats.

- Place dry food inside a muffin tin, then cover with tennis balls.

- Place dry food inside a brown paper lunch bag and crinkle it up.

- Place dry food inside an empty shoebox, then fill with ping-pong balls.

EASY STORE-BOUGHT PUZZLES:

- The LickiMat is great for wet food and takes quite a while for your cat to eat without being too difficult.

- Snuffle mats simulate rooting through grass to find food and are great for beginner kitties.

- The Digger by Catit is just what the name implies. Try this one out if you have a cat who loves to kick litter out of his box!

- The Catch Interactive Feeder can be used for wet or dry food and is easily thrown in the dishwasher when you're done.

- The Catit Senses Food Maze is on the more difficult end of the easy puzzles. It's a tall tower, and your cat must knock dry food or treats down each level to get to the bottom.

- The Trixie Cat Activity Feeder is my all-time favorite food puzzle for cats. It's on the pricier side but has five puzzles to solve all in one board. My cats will work on it for hours! Some pieces are only usable for dry food, but the "ice cube tray" portion can hold wet food as well.

There are unlimited ways to make mealtimes more fun and exciting for your cats with a little bit of creativity. After you've exhausted the easy choices

Photo Courtesy
of Lisa Flanery

with your cats, up the ante and see what you can do to make it a little more challenging each time. Just like you rotate your cat's toys, rotate the puzzles you offer so that your cat is always working his brain. Combined with two interactive play sessions a day, adding food puzzles to your cat's routine can resolve behavior issues such as nighttime party hour, play aggression, excessive meowing or demanding, attention-seeking behaviors, and more.

Outdoor Enrichment

If you recall, in Chapter 1, we had a lively debate on whether or not cats should have access to the outdoors. We landed on the conclusion that cats are safest when kept indoors, with controlled outdoor access provided as enrichment. I covered a few simple tips for enriching your indoor cat's life then, but I will fully elaborate on that now.

Harness training and leash walking are on almost every cat owner's list of things to try with their cat. After all, walking your cat on a leash allows him to explore to his heart's content while keeping him from darting out into the street and being hit by a car or getting spooked and hiding somewhere out of your reach. However, for most cat owners, the experience goes as follows: you wrestle kitty into a harness against his will, and he immediately flops over, throws a temper tantrum, and refuses to move. You pick him up and take him outside, where he immediately awkwardly crab-walks as fast as he can back towards the door, probably meowing desperately throughout. You say, "well, he hates the harness and being outside," and you put the harness and leash away in a drawer, never to be seen again. You're laughing because you literally had that exact experience with your cat, am I right?

Photo Courtesy of Katrina Ooms

Cats can't be expected to learn to tolerate wearing a harness in one session. Likewise, if your cat has spent his entire life indoors, of course, he's going to freak out when he gets outside! He is flooded with sights, sounds, and smells he's never been exposed to before. He has never felt grass under his paws. It's like being blind and suddenly being able to see. It takes gradual, slow desensitization to get a cat used to both wearing a harness and going outdoors. It could take days, weeks, or months before you're going on a walk around the neighborhood. Of course, it's always easier to start this process when your cat is a kitten. Before planning to take your cat outside for any length of time, be sure that he is up to date on vaccines and flea and tick preventative.

STEP BY STEP HARNESS TRAINING:

1. Leash walking first requires that the cat get used to wearing a harness. I recommend an "H" style harness as they are lightweight and difficult to back out of.

2. Begin by draping the harness (without the leash) over the cat's back. Keep the harness there for one second, then remove it. Give your cat a treat.

3. Continue to build up the time that the cat feels the weight of the harness draped over his back.

4. When that becomes boring, fasten the collar of the harness around the cat's neck. Allow the cat to wear it for a few seconds, giving him lots of treats, then remove it.

5. Gradually build up to the point where the cat is comfortable having the entire harness clipped on. This process will take several days or weeks as the cat adjusts to the strange feeling of the harness on his body. Remember to profusely reward your cat for tolerating the harness.

6. When the cat is completely comfortable wearing the harness and can move and walk normally while wearing it, you can add the leash. At first, clip the leash onto the harness and allow the cat to get used to the feeling of the leash dragging behind him.

7. Cats will not walk on a leash exactly like a dog might, but you can get the cat used to gentle leash pressure indoors first. Keep sessions short, practicing leash walking for about 5-10 minutes at a time.

8. If you plan to walk your cat outdoors, remember to keep the sessions short and at your cat's pace and be careful not to flood him if he is nervous. Allow your cat to make the choice to venture outdoors and allow slow desensitization to scary things he may encounter like large trucks, sirens, or dogs. It may be helpful to play a tape of outdoor or

*Photo Courtesy
of Donna Brown*

city noises indoors so that the cat becomes desensitized to sounds before going outside.

If harness training isn't right for you and your cat, maybe backpacking is or going for a walk in a pet stroller! Cats can learn to really enjoy these as well. The same care should be taken to allow your cat time to adjust to being in the backpack or stroller. Introduce him over several days using lots of treats and praise and gradually get him used to being enclosed inside. The more positive you make the experience, the more likely he is to feel comfortable when going outdoors. Start slow with just five minutes at a time out in the yard, and watch your cat carefully for signs of stress, like dilated pupils, meowing, or panting. It's important to remember that he won't simply just "get over" his fear if you keep going. At the first sign of stress, go back inside, let him out, and try again the next day, going back a step if necessary.

Pop-up tents and playpens can also work well for keeping cats safe outdoors. Get in the habit of taking kitty out with you outside in his playpen while you garden or do yard work. He can watch the birds, feel the fresh air, and smell all the scents from a comfy bed in his enclosure, all while spending time with you. Even better, if you have the room and the finances, build your cat his own "catio." Catios are a pun on patios and are outdoor enclosures designed for your cats to be able to go outside but stay confined. You may also want to look into cat fencing, such as the Purrfect Fence, which is designed specifically to keep cats inside your yard and prevent escape while making it extremely difficult for other animals to get in.

If all else fails, at the very least, you can always bring the outdoors in to your cat. Have you ever noticed that the moment you crack open a window in your home, your cats all flock to it? Peeking out an open window, feeling the air, and smelling the breeze can be very enriching for indoor cats. Bonus points if you crack the window for even a few minutes in the winter or summer, as your cat is likely used to a comfortable 72 degrees inside your home and rarely has the chance to feel heat or cold. Plant cat grass, catnip, or spider plants, and keep them inside for your cat to chew on (just don't let him eat too much). Add a small water feature or fountain with constant running water for him to sip on. Did it snow last night? Take a dishpan and fill it with a few inches of snow at the bottom, then scatter treats on top for your cat to explore. Hang a bird feeder near your window for your cat to watch. Get creative, and your cat will thank you for it.

Vertical Space

The last type of enrichment worth mentioning is providing your cat with plenty of vertical space to climb and explore. Cats are unique in that they are both predators and prey animals. We've talked a lot about satisfying the predator's need to forage and hunt through food puzzles and play therapy, but on the other end of the spectrum, the prey animal inside the cat needs vertical space. Why? From up high, cats can survey their surroundings and get a much better overall picture than if they were on the ground. Having lots of options to get up high can make a world of difference in your cat's confidence level and help them feel safe and secure.

Vertical space also increases the square footage your kitty has access to as well, giving them more resting places, spots to get away from children or other pets, and expanding their territory. Encouraging your cats to climb provides them with easy exercise, too. And, as an added bonus, the more appropriate places you provide for your cat to get up high, the less time he'll spend on your kitchen table and countertops. Here's how to create vertical space in your home:

- **Cat trees:** These are the most obvious way to create vertical space. I know that they're an eyesore. They don't match your décor. But these days, there are SO many on the market, from the most basic to the most elaborate possible, in every color scheme, height, and design you can imagine. And remember all the benefits they provide for your cats. Cat trees should be placed in higher-traffic areas of the home, where you and your cat spend a lot of your time. Put yourself inside your cat's shoes when deciding the proper placement. Does the highest point place your cat at a good vantage point? Can your cat see the front door to wait for you to get home? Watch you cooking in the kitchen? Survey the living room while you're on the couch watching TV?

FUN FACT
Toy Rotation

Toy rotation is a technique to prevent your cat from getting bored with its toys. The idea is to rotate your cat's toys several times a month. Some cat owners rotate groups of toys in and out, while others rotate one toy at a time. Then, store the unused toys in an inaccessible place and watch your cat go wild for its "new" toy each time you rotate!

- **Shelving:** Whether DIY or fancy cat furniture, shelving is ideal because it doesn't take up too much space and doesn't have to be expensive. Create a kitty super-highway around a room and get the added bonus of free entertainment as you watch your cat play acrobat, jumping from shelf to shelf.

- **Window perches:** I have a bay window at the front of my house. I'm not going to lie. That window was a huge selling point when I decided to move in. Since then, I have dressed it up with soft blankets and cozy beds and toys that suction cup to the window. During the winter, I'll plug in the heating pad under the blankets. It's quickly become the most well-loved, highly-trafficked resting place for my cats. Not only can they hang out with me in the living room, but they are well-elevated above the ground and have the perfect view of my front yard, complete with a bird feeder hanging from the tree. If you're not lucky enough to have a bay window to give to your cats, you can purchase resting places that hang from suction cups or attach to the wall to give your cat a comfortable lounging place to rest up high and watch out the window for you to come home.

Of note, though not necessarily a form of enrichment, hiding spots are also important for satisfying the needs of the prey animal inside your cat. Lots of boxes, hidey holes, and places to duck inside and under are essential for keeping him feeling safe and secure.

ADVICE FROM THE EXPERTS

What are some great ways to provide playtime and enrichment for your cat?

Play with your cat several times a day for 10–15 minutes. It stimulates the cat's mind and makes it happier. Cats are born to hunt, so find the 'style' of your cat and cater to it. Is your cat a bird catcher (likes to leap after toys) or a mouse hunter (likes to chase toys dragged along the floor)? Find the style and play with it!"

MARGARET SLABY
Golden Oldies Cat Rescue

Many cats love cat tunnels! Bring one out occasionally and toss toys through it for the cat to chase. Also use brown packing paper! We keep a big box of it in the living room and every now and then take some out and let the cats play in a pile of it."

LIZ OSTEN
Cat Rescue of Marlborough and Hudson (CaRMaH)

Fun things to keep your kitty entertained are fly toys, cat wheels, and puzzles. You can put out bird feeders for bird watching. Also, putting ping-pong balls in the tub can be fun for hours."

KATIE JOHNSON
Actually Rescuing Cats

Fishing pole–type toys are interactive (yes, cats know the owner is at the other end). Chasing a laser light (it doesn't get stuck on claws), scratching posts, empty cardboard boxes (a must for any cat owner!), fuzzy mice, jingle balls, wadded-up paper balls, empty toilet paper rolls—anything that can be batted around and knocked under the fridge!"

SANDY, CO-FOUNDER
(CLAWS) Cats Lives Are Worth Saving

“ *Remember to encourage play with toys and not your hands. Using your hands to play with younger cats and kittens will encourage them to play rough with you. Utilize wands, strings, balled-up pieces of paper, etc. Cats aren't picky when it comes to having a good time! Most of them will think they've hit the jackpot when they find empty shoeboxes and paper bags.”*

ELIZABETH FUDGE
Companion Animal Alliance

“ *There are so many ideas: cat grass, catnip. Build an outdoor enclosure for the cat with a tunnel back to the house via a cat door. Flapping fish are so fun to watch the cats stalk and pounce. Build an obstacle course and teach your cat to jump, crawl, and go through and over things.”*

LYNDA STREEPER
Humane Society of Northern Virginia

“ *Doing chores at home? (i.e., walking back and forth to do the dishes, laundry, etc.) Well, tie a string to your waist with a toy at the end. Voilà! You are a human kitty toy! Your cat will chase you around to get the toy at the end of the string.”*

LINDA DIAMOND
SoBe Cats Spay & Neuter, Inc.

“ *We love the interactive puzzles and activity centers that double as a hunting experience for your cat. Cats are hunters, and even though they are now domesticated, they still enjoy the thrill of the hunt, even if it's just a few kibbles of food! These interactive puzzles for cat food or treats allow your pets to work for a treat while exercising that natural instinct they have.”*

AMANDA HODDER
Kitten Rescue Life

“ *Every cat, just like every human, likes different types of play. Most cats will enjoy play that imitates hunting. Wand toys are great for this! I have yet to find a cat that doesn't love a cat dancer. They will play for hours on end! Interactive playtime is very important for health and mental stimulation. Your cat will get exercise, bond further with you, and not be bored. A bored cat is more likely to get into trouble.”*

CORI LYNN STANLEY
Averting CAT-astrophe

" *Set aside quality time each day to play with your cat. If you are using a laser pointer, remember that cats not only like the hunt, but they also like the capture. If you just have your cat chasing a laser pointer with no reward, this will result in an anxious and upset cat. Place stuffed animals or toys around the room. Let the cat chase the laser and then land on a toy for it to 'kill.' Continue on with the chase and the kill, and the kitty will have had an enjoyable playtime."*

MARILEE WELLS
Maricats Rescue

CHAPTER 9

Saying Goodbye: A Lifetime Commitment

Although this book is about preparing to adopt a new cat, it wouldn't feel complete without a chapter on caring for your senior cat and knowing when to say goodbye. Whether you pull this book out again 20 years after adopting your kitten or six months after adopting a 15-year-old cat from a shelter, death will always be a part of that circle of life. Cats are living longer

Photo Courtesy
of Michele Fellows

and longer these days, thanks to better nutrition and vet care. My oldest cat lived to be 27 years old (although that is not the norm). Generally, cats are thought to become seniors at around age 11, converting to "super senior" by age 15.

I'm a huge, huge supporter of adopting senior cats. There are lots of excuses not to, and that's why they tend to sit in shelters longer. Often, a shel-

FUN FACT
The Oldest Cat

According to Guinness World Records, the oldest recorded cat was Creme Puff. Creme Puff was born on August 3, 1967, and died 38 years and three days later. Another long-lived feline named Rubble lived a whopping 31 years and passed away in Exeter in 2020.

ter cage and the stress of losing their home will hit seniors harder than younger cats. They may hide, cower, or hiss in their cages, giving potential adopters the false idea that they are not friendly. In fact, they are just extremely stressed and need your help desperately to feel safe, loved, and comfortable again.

REASONS TO ADOPT A SENIOR CAT:

- **You know what you're getting:** no surprises! When you pick out that cute, snuggly, playful eight-week-old kitten, you have no idea what he'll turn out to be like in a few years. Yes, how you raise your cat plays a role in his personality but so does genetics. He may be snuggly now, but when he grows up, you may not have that lap cat anymore. With a senior cat, what you see is what you get. Many are lower energy and more tuned in to their humans. They've outgrown any destructive or annoying behaviors, and they're much more low maintenance.

- **Reality check:** 15–20 years is a huge commitment for anyone to take on. If you plan to move, start a family, travel, or whatever the case may be in the future, are you ready to take your kitten with you for the next decade? If not, an older cat may be a perfect fit. Maybe it's macabre, but if you're only talking five years instead of 15, a senior may be better for your lifestyle.

- **Senior cats are good for humans of all ages.** I hear a lot about programs designed to help match senior cats with senior humans, which is awesome! Grandma and Grandpa are going to be much happier with their low-energy, calm 12-year-old cat, who spends most of his days curled up on the couch, than they will be with a crazy six-month-old kitten who needs constant attention and supervision. I adopted my first senior cat when I was in my early 20s, and that was great for me too. I was finishing up school, working full time, and just crazy busy in general. My old man, Thomas, was happy and content to go with the flow as long as his food bowl was never empty and he had a soft, warm cat bed to snooze the day away.

- **You're doing a good thing.** Senior cats are less likely to be adopted, point-blank. In a shelter environment, a longer stay and a weaker immune system mean that seniors are more likely to get sick and more likely to become or remain very stressed, meaning that they won't show well to adopters. After all, are you more likely to go for the friendly cat reaching his paw through the bars to touch you or the catatonic lump hiding under his bed in the back of the cage? Just because this is how a cat presents in a shelter cage does not mean this is how he will be in your home. It just means he needs you even more!

Okay, I hear what you're saying. It's too sad to adopt a senior! I can't afford the vet bills that come with an older cat! But guess what? Kittens get old, too. Yes, I can acknowledge that adopting a senior cat isn't for everyone. But for me, the rewards that come with saving a life and choosing a less desirable cat outweigh the sadness that comes along with your cat slowing down and coming down with health issues.

I adopted my first senior, Thomas, from a shelter when he was 26 years old. His owner had passed away, and the family was not able to take on his advanced needs. Thomas lived another year and a half after I brought him home, and that short time period with him was truly an honor. Knowing that I gave him dignity in his old age and a safe retirement home where he was loved was so rewarding for me. Of course, I was devastated when he was diagnosed with cancer, and we had to say goodbye, but I'd do it all over again in a heartbeat simply for the honor of knowing him.

When we get into vet bills and overall cost, I'd also like to debunk the myth that senior cats cost more. Okay, there's no getting around that they require more frequent vet visits and are overall more prone to health problems. But a cat of any age can have a medical emergency. Cats can become diabetic at only a few years old, or develop a cardiac issue, or jump down from a shelf the wrong way and break a leg. Kittens tend to have higher adoption fees than adult cats, and often, shelters and rescues will waive adoption fees entirely for seniors.

Even if your adopted senior cat has a chronic medical condition, such as hyperthyroidism, which is extremely common in older cats, daily medication will only run you about $10–20 a month. And some shelters and rescues will

offer "Forever Foster" programs for senior cats where they continue to pay for the cat's vet bills for the rest of his life. Do your research, but don't be scared off. Give a senior cat a chance!

Senior Cat Care

Now that I've had a chance to convince you to adopt an older cat, we should cover the types of specialized care that he may need. Certain health conditions are more common in senior cats, and it's important to be able to recognize when your cat needs vet care, as these conditions often present as or are misinterpreted as behavioral problems. Pay especially close attention to changes in your cat's behavior, such as urinating outside of the litter box, any change in his routine like failing to greet you at the door when you come home, excessive meowing, signs of distress such as wandering aimlessly, reduced or increased appetite, or anything else out of the ordinary. Knowing your cat and his routines and habits well will be instrumental in addressing any health conditions quickly and efficiently.

Common Senior Cat Health Problems:

- **Hyperthyroidism:** This is the big one, affecting roughly 20 percent of all cats over the age of ten and making it the most common health problem in older cats. It can present in a variety of different ways, so generally, if your cat is acting differently than he usually does, it's a good idea to have his thyroid checked. Common signs include significantly increased appetite, increased thirst, weight loss even if eating more than usual, increased urination with possible accidents outside of the box, increased vocalization—particularly at night, vomiting, and irritability.

Your vet will run a blood test to confirm and will likely prescribe daily medication in pill form, as this is the cheapest way of treating the issue. If your vet prescribes methimazole, you can also ask for it in liquid or transdermal form.

Regular bloodwork will be necessary for cats suffering from hyperthyroidism to ensure that the medication is still working and does not need to be adjusted. Other treatments are available, including a prescription diet for mild cases. Surgical removal of the thyroid gland or radioactive iodine treatment are also options. Although more invasive and more expensive, these treatments can permanently resolve hyperthyroidism without the need for lifelong medication.

- **Arthritis:** If you have a senior cat, he probably has some kind of arthritis pain. What is commonly thought to be just your cat slowing down in his old age is actually more likely to be pain-related. Signs of arthritis include reluctance or hesitation to jump up on furniture, difficulty with stairs, difficulty getting in and out of the litter box, reduced activity, and limping or stiffness. Overweight and declawed cats are more prone to arthritis, too. Your vet may recommend NSAIDs or a joint supplement such as Dasuquin. In addition, you can help your cat out by giving him an electric blanket or heated bed to sleep in, providing him with a low-entry litter box such as the Kitty Go Here senior cat box, placing everything he needs at floor level or providing him with ramps or pet stairs, and helping him to maintain a healthy weight.

- **Diabetes:** The most common symptoms that owners will notice may be peeing outside the litter box, increased hunger and thirst, increased urine volume, weight loss, and/or a greasy coat. If your cat is experiencing any of these, your vet will likely recommend bloodwork (complete blood count and chemistry), a urinalysis, and fructosamine testing. Some cats will require insulin; others may have their diabetes controlled by diet alone. Your vet will be able to help you choose the right treatment strategy for your cat. Generally, all diabetic cats do best on a diet of canned food only, the most commonly recommended brand being Fancy Feast pate, if not prescription food from your vet.

A diagnosis of diabetes can be scary for many cat owners, as it involves careful monitoring, frequent testing, and in some cases, giving your cat daily shots of insulin. In addition to working closely with your vet, there are many resources that can help you if your cat is diagnosed with diabetes, including Diabetic Cats in Need, a nonprofit group providing education, financial assistance, and rehoming support to owners of diabetic cats.

- **Kidney disease:** Common signs that your cat may be suffering from chronic kidney disease (CKD) include lethargy, excessive thirst and urination, unkempt appearance, and weight loss. There is no cure for CKD, and it involves the gradual loss of kidney function over time, ultimately resulting in death. Fortunately, it can be well-controlled, and many cats with CKD live many years after their diagnosis. Your vet will run bloodwork and a urinalysis before deciding on a treatment plan. Usually, your cat will be placed on a prescription diet, and he may require fluid therapy on a regular basis to make sure he stays adequately hydrated. With subcutaneous fluid therapy, your vet will show you how to place a needle under your cat's skin at home to release fluids under his skin. In some cases, intravenous fluid therapy may be required, which will require regular trips to the vet.

- **Dental disease:** Two of my cats that I adopted as seniors had to have full mouth extractions done where they lost all of their teeth! This is not uncommon, and almost every single cat will need to have dental work done at some point in his life. Look for your cat pawing at his mouth, eating less or having trouble eating, drooling excessively, or having bad breath beyond normal stinky tuna breath after he's eaten. Many times, these signs are missed, which is why it's extremely important to take your cat to the vet at least annually. If your cat gets regular dental cleanings throughout his life, this will pay off long-term. Often, cats don't receive dental care until it's too late, and they will require extractions of teeth on top of a thorough cleaning under sedation. Left untreated, dental disease can affect other parts of your cat's body and has been linked to heart, liver, and kidney disease.

- **Sensory loss and feline dementia:** Just like humans, cats aren't as sharp as they used to be in their old age. Many cats lose sensory function and may have trouble hearing or seeing over the years. It's important to bring your older cats indoors, as sensory loss makes them more vulnerable to predators and other dangers that the outdoors bring on. Cats may also decline cognitively as they reach old age, and you may notice confusion, litter box accidents, lack of self-grooming, anxiety, irritability, restlessness, increased vocalization, changes in sleep cycle, or really any change in behavior. About 50 percent of cats over the age of 15 will experience some symptoms of cognitive decline. There's not much that can be done in this situation – just remember that although some of these behavioral changes may be frustrating, it's not your cat's fault. He needs your love and support now more than ever.

- **Cancer:** The big "C" word – it's the leading cause of death in cats. Weight loss, vomiting, diarrhea, lack of appetite, and discomfort are all common, as well as the more obvious visible tumor on your cat's body. Symptoms can vary from cat to cat and between types of cancer – just another reason to keep a close eye on your senior cat's behavior to notice any subtle change. Bloodwork, radiographs, ultrasounds, MRIs, and CT scans can all be used to diagnose cancer in cats, as well as aspiration or biopsy. Your vet may recommend chemotherapy, surgical removal, or consulting with

*Photo Courtesy
of Heather Greenberg*

a feline oncologist. In some cases, the best treatment for you and your cat may be no treatment at all, simply focusing on the time you have left together and keeping your feline friend as comfortable as possible for the rest of his days.

This is not a comprehensive list of medical issues that could arise in your cat, but they are some of the most commonly seen ones. Pay very close attention to your senior cat, and note any behavioral changes so that you can address any health concerns early on.

Accommodating Your Senior Cat

I briefly touched on this when discussing arthritis in cats, but your senior cat is going to eventually slow down, and getting around may be difficult or painful for him during those last couple of years. Keep that in mind and consider making a few special accommodations in his final years to make things easier on your cat and give him a better quality of life.

- Senior cats generally need more help with grooming. Keeping your cat's nails trimmed regularly and brushing him once or twice a week will make a big difference. Be sure to keep things gentle, especially if you're dealing with any mats. If your cat's coat becomes unkempt beyond what you're able to handle, consulting with a professional groomer that comes to your home may be necessary.

- By now, you know all about proper litter box choice and placement. It's especially important to consider these choices in senior cats. Your 15-year-old cat can't hold his bladder like he used to, and he certainly can't be expected to make it all the way down the basement stairs in time. Keep litter boxes on every floor, near where your cat spends most of his time. Look for a box that is easy for him to step into – I recommend the Kitty Go Here, which can be found on Amazon. In very elderly cats, you may have to get creative with cutting out extra low entry points or even try out a crate tray so that your cat does not have to lift up his legs to step in and out of the box. In super seniors, puppy pads will be your best friend. Litter box accidents are probably going to happen, so do your best to set up your old guy or gal for success.

- You may notice your cat becoming pickier about his food and water in his old age. Try offering his food and water in different types of bowls. Consider a water fountain. Add water, tuna juice, or chicken broth to his food to soften it up and add extra taste. Try heating up canned food in the microwave. Offer multiple consistencies and multiple brands. Sitting with your cat and encouraging him to eat can make a difference, too. If inappetence persists, have your vet check him out. They may be able to prescribe an appetite stimulant.

FUN FACT
Grooming a Senior Cat

Senior cats may begin to have difficulty grooming themselves and require extra care from you. Gentle grooming can help prevent matting in long-haired cats and can be a meaningful bonding experience for you and your cat. However, in some cases, senior cats will still develop matting and should be taken to a groomer to be shaved for their comfort.

- Remember that your cat isn't getting around like he used to. If you're able to provide everything to him on one floor so that he doesn't have to use stairs in order to get to his food or litter box, this is ideal. Offer ramps or pet stairs so that he doesn't have to take a big jump to get to the couch or bed. Adding rugs to tile, hardwood, or laminate floor areas can be helpful, especially if you have stairs of this material. Your cat may not want to stretch up to scratch anymore, so offering horizontal scratching items can be helpful. Make your home as senior-friendly as possible!

- Your elderly cat may not play like he used to, and that's okay. Slow down his play sessions with easier "prey," but don't stop play entirely. He may have been able to jump into the air to grab a toy before, but now, he's probably much more content to bat at it while lying on his side.

- I mentioned it briefly earlier, but heated beds are like magic for old cats. Offer a heating pad, electric blanket, or heated cat bed, and watch your elderly cat gravitate to it instantly. It's cozy and comfortable and also soothes his achy old bones.

End of Life and Hospice Care: How Do You Know When It's Time?

There will come a time in your relationship with your cat where you start to question his quality of life. How do you make that big decision to say goodbye to your best friend and steady companion? Newsflash: it will always come sooner than you expect and long before you're ready. My biggest advice is that you'll know when it's time. You just will. Even if you adopted an 18-year-old cat with kidney disease, and now you're faced with that decision after only a couple of months, you are the person who knows your cat best. You are his best advocate and the person best equipped to know what the best decision is for him. It definitely doesn't always feel that way, but it's true.

Photo Courtesy of Katrina Ooms

I recommend using a veterinarian who specializes in hospice and end-of-life services if you're still not confident that you're able to know when it's time on your own. Lap of Love is an amazing resource with veterinary hospice services located in most states across the USA. These vets will come to visit your cat at home to help you come up with a plan for hospice care and eventual peaceful passage. Lap of Love, as well as other local hospice care veterinary organizations, will usually come prepared with their version of a Quality-of-Life scale to help you make a determination. Scales differ across different organizations, but personally, I like to look at seven different aspects of your cat's behavior and health:

- **Mobility:** How is your cat getting around? Can he use stairs, jump up on furniture, and stand up from lying down without major difficulty? Is he spending most of his time in one spot, or is he moving from place to place as usual? Does he need help to do some of the things he used to, or is he no longer even attempting?

- **Food intake:** Is he eating more or less than usual? Has he stopped eating entirely? Can you entice him with special treats or people food, but he won't touch anything else? Does he only eat when you're sitting with him petting him? Has he lost significant weight despite eating regular meals?

- **Water intake:** Is he drinking a ton, or has he not touched his water bowl recently? Either extreme can be a bad sign.

- **Personality and favorite things:** Is your cat usually the life of the party and the first one to meet you at the door when you come home? Maybe, despite being a senior, he enjoys a good game of fetch and an occasional chase of the feather wand. Maybe he's a lap cat or an avid bird watcher. Whatever your cat's normal behavior is, is he still doing those things? Does he spend all his time sleeping and won't wake up even for the crinkle of the treat bag opening? Simply put, is your cat still enjoying life like he used to?

- **Urination/defecation habits:** Too much, not enough, diarrhea, accidents outside of the box – all of these are causes for concern but aren't alone a reason to think that things have progressed beyond repair. When your cat starts to pee in his bed or right where he is lying or isn't making it to his litter box 50 percent or more of the time, we start to worry more about incontinence, which is a quality-of-life concern.

- **Medical management:** If your cat's medical issue was well-controlled with medication or whatever treatment plan you and your vet discussed, but now it isn't, we have to start thinking about quality of life. If this chronic condition is no longer being managed or responding to treatment, your cat may be suffering.

- **Physical presentation.** Is he unkempt or dirty? Does he have any open sores, lumps or bumps, or tumors? Is he disoriented, confused, distressed, or having difficulty breathing? Is he crying out in pain? Any of these may be signs of an emergency.

These are guidelines and things to think about, nothing more. However, if you have observed several of these behaviors or signs in your cat, discuss it with your vet, and start coming to terms with the fact that a difficult decision may be in your future. A good rule of thumb is to have that discussion once your cat seems to have more bad days than good days.

Euthanasia isn't and shouldn't be a dirty word. It means intentionally ending life in order to relieve pain and suffering. It's giving your cat a peaceful, dignified ending, recognizing that there is no perfect moment and that the right time may feel different from person to person. Many cat owners want to be able to give their cat a perfect last day, doing his favorite things and eating his favorite meal, preventing him from feeling any intense suffering at all. Other cat owners want to hold on until the last moment, spending every possible second with their friend as possible and taking longer to come to terms with the decision. There is no right or wrong answer.

Humane euthanasia is a gift you give to your cat and shouldn't make you feel guilty or immoral. When performed in order to relieve a pet of pain and suffering, it's the most responsible, humane decision you can make for your cat in the end. Although it's possible that your cat may pass peacefully in his sleep on his own, many times, a natural death can be painful and involve prolonged suffering. Although I recognize that it's a personal decision and not one that everyone can cope with, please consider having your pet's euthanasia done at home or going back into the room with him at your vet's office. Your cat needs you in his final moments, which can be scary and lonely for him if all he has for comfort is an, albeit kind, stranger.

When you do make that final decision, don't be shy about asking your veterinarian any questions you may have about the process. Most vets can accommodate special requests, like if you want to hold your cat in your lap instead of having him rest on the exam table. Generally, your vet will first give your cat a sedative to make him fall asleep. Once he is calm and relaxed, the vet will then administer the lethal injection. It is a quick, painless process, which causes your cat's heartbeat to slow down and eventually stop. Your cat peacefully drifts away, usually within seconds of the injection. You will likely be offered the choice to take his body home for burial or be given the option to have his body cremated. Most vets will offer private cremation, where you would receive his ashes back in an urn or wooden box to display. You may also choose mass cremation, where your cat will be cremated along with other animals and his ashes disposed of respectfully.

Dealing with Loss

This is a difficult topic and one I don't have all the answers to. I will say that you're not alone and that you're absolutely normal if you struggle to cope with the loss of a pet. It's true that losing a pet can sometimes be more traumatic than or comparable to losing a human family member. You're losing a source of unconditional love, comfort, and companionship, as well as a being whose life depended on and revolved around you, almost like a child. I think it's okay to feel that way about a cat or a dog.

There can be a stigma around coping with the loss of a cat, right? Is it socially acceptable to miss work because your cat died? Can you burst out crying around your friends weeks later because you saw a cat on TV that looked like yours without getting a weird look? I don't know. I guess it depends on your employer and your friends. I will say that I think both of those things are just fine. I wouldn't judge you. It's hard. It may get easier with time, and it may not. You may decide to get a new cat in the future, and you may not. I want to point out that people grieve differently, and that's okay too. You might be so upset at that empty feeling in your home that you want to adopt another cat a week after your cat's passing. You also may need to wait a few months or a year before you feel ready. Both options are okay.

For me, it helps to save something in memory of my pet who has passed. It could be an ink or clay pawprint offered by my vet, a box containing his ashes, a photograph, a favorite toy, collar, or whatever you think honors and preserves your cat's memory the best. I have dealt with a lot of loss over the years, as I tend to gravitate towards bringing home senior cats or cats in need of hospice care. I have a set of shelves in the corner of my bedroom that houses all these memorial items I have saved. Talking about your cat helps too. I'm a writer, obviously, and I talk about and write down favorite memories and how we managed to make each other's lives better and more complete. Whatever helps you grieve is okay, and you should never feel ashamed for doing so. No matter what happens or what your situation is, you made your cat's life as happy as you possibly could, and that's what matters in the end.

ADVICE FROM THE EXPERTS

What's your best advice for caring for a senior cat during its golden years?

Regular vet checks with bloodwork are essential to catch things that will happen early (such as kidney disease). Be patient and understand that the cat sometimes might not make it to the litter box. JUST LOVE YOUR CAT. It has been with you and has given you its love. Please do not get rid of it because it is old!"

MARGARET SLABY
Golden Oldies Cat Rescue

Trust your vet or find one that you trust. Go to the vet at least yearly, if not twice yearly. As prey animals, cats will hide illness from you until it's way late in the game. Frequent exams will allow your vet a chance to uncover issues early on so that you can address them and reduce suffering."

LIZ OSTEN
Cat Rescue of Marlborough and Hudson (CaRMaH)

Once cats become seniors, they should be kept on any medication the vet suggests, and you should follow vet orders to care for whatever condition they may have. Cats lose the ability to clean themselves well as they age. You can brush them more and use pet wipes to clean them a few times a week."

JULIA MELTON
Summit Animal Rescue Assn.

Pay attention to cats' eating/drinking/bathroom habits. Give them lots of love and warm laps to nap on! If the time comes that you need to make a decision, work with your vet to educate yourself on your cat's condition, and make the humane one if needed. It's in our nature to selfishly want to keep our pets with us, but it's not always the best for them."

LESLIE THOMAS
Itty Bitty Kitty Committee

“ *Keep the house calm and let seniors take their catnaps in peace. Make sure they have healthy teeth (often overlooked by owners). Give them extra wet food (great for their kidneys) and love, love, love on them."*

LINDA DIAMOND
SoBe Cats Spay & Neuter, Inc.

“ *Treat senior cats as you would want to be treated is my best advice. Feline bodies change over time, just as human bodies do. There's no telling how and how fast these things will progress! Provide love, attention, and thoughtful care, keeping in mind your kitty might be losing its sharp eyesight, keen hearing, and the easy, graceful movements it previously had."*

ELIZABETH FUDGE
Companion Animal Alliance

“ *Adopting a senior is extremely rewarding. To give a cat a home for his golden years is an awesome thing. If it's your own cat, it may get messier than it was. It may get crankier or have minor health issues. It's part of it, and your cat needs you now more than ever. We get a lot of surrender requests for older cats whose issues could likely be solved with a quick vet visit to see what is causing the new behavior."*

KIM KAY
Angels Among Us Pet Rescue

“ *Senior cats deserve lots of peace and comfort. Try to not make huge changes in the home like adding a new pet or leaving the home for long hours or days at a time. Take them in for senior checkups every six to 12 months. Make sure they are up to date on any dental work needed and do routine bloodwork to make sure they are in their peak health."*

AMANDA HODDER
Kitten Rescue Life

“ *Senior cats are masters at hiding health issues, and a blood test will help keep the liver and kidneys monitored. Watch for signs of arthritis. Remember the eyesight and hearing might be fading. Give cats attention when they want it. Time passes so fast."*

ANNA SEALS
Central Indiana Foster Cats

> " *Pay attention to your cat's changing needs! Cats' nutritional needs change as they get older. Weight fluctuations and general coat condition are great ways to monitor this. Senior pets need a little extra help. Steps to get up on the bed or the couch may be necessary. A low-sided litter pan will make it easier for your cat to get in and out. Also, litter type may need to change for your cat's comfort and stability. Ask your vet about nutritional supplements and supplements for joint health. And pay attention to smells! Stinky breath, ears, and coat or changes in potty smells can indicate that treatment is necessary! Catch problems early, and they are more likely to be treatable. Most importantly, keep loving your cat! You are everything to it, and it depends on you! It is hard to watch cats age, but as long as they have a good quality of life, they will be happy being loved and cared for by their forever person.*"

CORI LYNN STANLEY
Averting CAT-astrophe

> " *I've found that older cats especially like being brushed. It's harder for them to groom themselves. Be aware of changes in eating habits or litter box habits and don't hesitate to talk to the vet if needed. Dental care is important. If you've been brushing your cat's teeth and he tolerate it, keep doing it, but be especially gentle. If not, schedule a dental cleaning at the vet. Encourage cats to play, but don't force it.*"

ROSEMARY TOROK
Community Cat Companions

> " *Learning how to give SQ fluids (subcutaneous fluid injections) is ESSENTIAL. Every cat owner who plans to have a cat live older than 10 needs to learn how to do SQ fluids. It is easy once taught, and life-saving. And your cat will feel and eat better when fluids are needed. The other advice is having a more easily accessible litter box. I had a senior cat who started peeing on my bed, and when I added a litter box to my bedroom, she stopped peeing on my bed. She just didn't want to walk any further anymore to go to the other litter box.*"

AVARIE SHEVIN
Stray Cat Alliance

> " If you live in a cold climate, heated cat beds are a great comfort to older, arthritic cats. Let them sleep. If they start hiding or sleeping in odd, out-of-the-way places, that can be a sign that something is wrong."

BETSY BALLENGER
Cat Action Team

> " Are cats having more difficulty getting on the couch or making it to the litter box? Raise dishes, lower litter boxes, provide stairs to the bed and couch. Take your kitty to the vet for suggestions on supplements for arthritis if it's developing. Watch your cat's weight. You might need to give more treats if it's not eating as much."

JOANNA LANDRUM
Rutherford County Cat Rescue

Epilogue

Well, we've reached the end of the book. I hope that you learned something, whether you are just thinking about adopting your first cat, have had a couple of cats in your life but want to learn how to be a better cat owner in the future, or are like my mom, who just bought this book out of obligation. When it comes to cats, there is never a point where you've learned everything there is to know about them. Cats are just beginning to be recognized as trainable, valuable pets in a world where dogs seem to take precedence. New research on how best to meet our cats' needs as pet owners and professionals is coming out every single day.

Something I hear a lot as a young person who happens to be a subject matter expert on cats and cat behavior is, "Oh honey, I've had cats longer than you've been alive," or, "I've been using a squirt bottle on cats for 20 years and I've never had an issue." I say to those people that experience is great, but education is what is truly important when it comes to caring for your cat. After all, would you go to a dentist whose only qualifications were that he has owned his teeth for the last 30 years? I hope that you wouldn't, and the moral of the story is, I'm glad you took the time to further your education in reading. Congratulations, and enjoy life with your cats.

Made in United States
Orlando, FL
02 February 2023

29340991R00096